CHRISTIANS
IN THE
CROSSFIRE

Guarding Your Mind Against
Manipulation and Self-deception

CHRISTIANS
IN THE
CROSSFIRE

Guarding Your Mind Against
Manipulation and Self-deception

BY

MARK McMINN & JAMES FOSTER

THE BARCLAY PRESS
Newberg, Oregon 97132

CHRISTIANS IN THE CROSSFIRE
Guarding Your Mind Against Manipulation and Self-deception

International Standard Book Number: 0-913342-68-8

Library of Congress Catalog Card Number: 90-82741

2 3 4 5 6 7 8 9 / 94 93 92 91

Cover by Wes Cropper and Steve Eichenberger

Interior design, composition, and lithography by
The Barclay Press, Newberg, Oregon 97132, U.S.A.

Contents

Acknowledgments

We are indebted to several who have helped us conceive, organize, and edit *Christians in the Crossfire*. Arthur Roberts and Gayle Beebe helped with their critiques of our initial outlines. Kin Millen's editing of the first and second drafts was so thorough that it was discouraging at first. But his suggestions were excellent and the book reflects his wisdom. Michelle Downing Barnhart and Lisa McMinn read the manuscript carefully and made helpful comments. Donna McMinn and Mark Ankeny, both committed Christians and public educators, made helpful suggestions on Chapter 9. Dan McCracken at Barclay Press has been encouraging and committed to this project. We appreciate the support and encouragement of our families.

Our faculty positions at George Fox College allow us the freedom to pursue scholarship and writing. More than time, we value the stimulating interactions with colleagues and opportunities for Christian growth coupled with intellectual integrity. Lee Nash, vice president for academic affairs, deserves credit for challenging the faculty to explore what it means to love God with our minds. Many other colleagues have modeled critical thinking in their academic disciplines and spiritual walk and have contributed to our thinking.

Introduction

Linda returned to college from Christmas vacation discouraged and with doubts about her major. She was an enthusiastic young Christian with a sincere desire to help suffering people. In order to do this Linda had decided to major in psychology. But during Christmas vacation some members of her church had warned her to avoid the field. Her friends were concerned about her faith.

Alan was unhappy because he felt the college he attended was tainted with secular humanism. Christian professors assigned textbooks written by secular authors, students attended chapel only three days a week, and the college had a psychology major. Alan transferred to a Bible college established by a popular TV evangelist. Students there believed as he did, there were few differing points of view, and most were devout followers of the school's founder. A short time later, the school's leader was involved in a sex scandal. We never heard from Alan again and can only wonder how he fared.

As college professors we come into contact with many Christian young people, like Linda and Alan, suffering from a kind of shell shock—a battle fatigue caused by living in the crossfire of ideas. Students struggle daily with questions that have no simple answers. Society bombards them with messages that promote one kind of lifestyle while our churches promote another. Even within the church there are mixed messages about sexuality, morality, and patriotism. In the midst of conflicting messages, young adults have to make innumerable decisions about what to wear, what to believe, what to think, and how to behave.

But the confusion isn't limited to students. We live in the shadow of an ideological Tower of Babel, bombarded by a bewildering variety of ideas, values, and beliefs. Modern life is life in an ideological war zone where we must sort through the myriad "truths" as we seek to follow Christ. And the decisions we make about what to believe and what to value have profound consequences for us and our children.

Answering questions and forming valid opinions is particularly difficult because we live in an information age. We are confronted with more information than we can possibly use, and the information we receive is often contradictory. "Send your children to public schools to prepare them for real life." "Educate your children at home and keep them away from secular humanism." "Send your children to Christian schools." "Don't let your children play with secular toys, watch TV, or listen to rock music." "Earn more money to provide for your family." "Do more volunteer work for your church." "Donate more." "Work less." "Work more."

This book is not about what to believe; there are many of those available. This is a book about standing firm in the midst of ideological crossfire, keeping our eyes on Christ as we use the discipline of critical thinking. As we prepared this book, we kept two goals in mind.

First, we are committed to the goal that Christians be excellent in their thinking skills. The Apostle Paul instructed the church at Thessalonica to "examine everything carefully; hold fast to that which is good; abstain from every form of evil." (1 Thessalonians 5:21, 22) Paul's words indicate that an essential element of distinguishing good from evil is to think clearly and critically about issues. Only as we think soundly can we come to appropriate decisions about good and evil. We can never delegate our thinking to others, regardless of how much we trust them. Paradoxically, we need others to help us recognize faulty ways of thinking. Throughout the book we present ways of careful thinking and ways we might easily fail to think carefully about critical issues facing Christians today.

Second, we desire to present critical thinking skills without bashing those who disagree with us on specific issues. We use specific examples of those who fall prey to thinking fallacies, and we have disagreed with many of our Christian brothers and sisters. But we do so while recognizing a responsibility to love those with whom we disagree. Christians have read enough books that bash other believers and other ways of believing. What we need now is détente—a way to sort through the rubble of battle and come up with the cherished prize of truth. And we need to remember to love one another in the process. Some of the crossfire is nothing more than a lack of clarity on the vocabulary Christians use. For example, when some authors write about humanism, they mean something entirely different from what others call humanism. Defining terms is an important first step in thinking critically about the issues we face as Christians. We've attempted to reduce this problem by defining the way we use some terms in the glossary at the end of the book.

Finally, we would like to offer a word of caution to our readers. Our goal is to help Christians develop the critical thinking skills necessary to live wise and godly lives in the midst of the ideological crossfire we see all around us. In writing such a book it is necessary to take positions and use illustrations. But in so doing there is a danger that readers will uncritically accept what we have to say. As we make suggestions for improving critical thinking abilities, remember to apply those suggestions to what we have written.

3

CHAPTER ONE

Christians Under Siege

Be careful that nobody spoils your faith through intellectualism or high-sounding nonsense. Colossians 2:8

There once was a time when Christians in the United States could say with confidence that they lived in a Christian nation. They lived and worked among people in their communities who accepted predominantly Christian standards of morality and integrity. The schools their children attended upheld their beliefs. A certain uniformity of thought and behavior permeated society. Exposure to other religions, belief systems, and standards of behavior was rare for most individuals. And people who happened to hold ideas that departed from that norm were often seen as suspect by the rest of the community. Those who wanted to flirt with other organized belief systems had to make a conscious effort to find them.

But the information age has changed this ideological isolation. Today it is impossible to function in society and *not* be exposed to a wide variety of ideas — ideas concerning where we came from, where we're going, and our purpose for living. Radio, cable and broadcast TV, the cinema and videocassette player, local and national newspapers and magazines, book publishing, schools, and even our own mobility have resulted in a much broader dispersion of widely differing values and beliefs than at any time in history. Today it takes no thought or effort to be thoroughly drenched, or even drowned, in the rough sea of ideas.

The information age has also created a climate of competition among the advocates of these philosophies. Each person or group with a cause competes for air time and media coverage. Some even compete for legislation that will be

5

advantageous for their cause. The spokespeople for these groups forcefully proclaim their right to be heard and their civil right to whatever objectives they are striving for. Frequently when their methods and objectives are criticized or exposed, they charge the same media they seek to use with distortion and lack of balance. Not content to withdraw from battle, they mount wave after wave of assault to be heard. And sometimes, because of their repeated offensives, they reach their goal either through public apathy or eventual persuasion.

For many Christians, life in the information age has become life on the battlefield of ideas. We are bombarded with philosophies and values opposed to our Christian beliefs. Daily we filter through our minds and reject messages that advocate the irreligious theories of the day and lifestyles that are anything but scripturally based. Many of these messages are openly hostile to Christianity and irreconcilable to a biblical lifestyle. These messages range from the seemingly harmless to the blatantly corrupt, profane, and ungodly.

David and Cheryl exemplify those affected by this crossfire of ideas. Married as Christians in a large church wedding, they seemed to be the ideal couple. Both came from strong Christian homes and had strong ties to godly values. But shortly after they were married, Cheryl began investigating the New Age Movement. Soon she stopped attending church because the "people were too dogmatic and pushy." By the third year of marriage, Cheryl was consulting mystical cards and astrological symbols to decide how to live her life. One night she abruptly announced that she had been seeing another man and that her symbols had confirmed she should divorce David and marry her new lover. David and Cheryl were casualties on the battlefield of ideas, and they are not alone.

6

The Frontal Attack

Many of the messages in which we are drowning make up a frontal attack on Christianity. They are in opposition to the things of God and usually come from those outside the Christian faith. These messages are threatening the vitality of many Christians' spiritual life, causing some to no longer be concerned with the things of Christ. Dr. Earl Radmacher, former president of Western Baptist Seminary, writes, "We have left the Age of Reason far behind and are living in what I choose to call the Age of Unreason."[1] In this age of unreason many Christians seem to be falling prey to opposing beliefs. Examples of attacks on our beliefs are numerous and diverse.

The New Age Movement. The New Age Movement has invaded the American way of life. It is a worldwide occult network, yet rather amorphous, of over 3,500 groups and organizations. Their goal is to bring in the New Age of humankind—the Age of Aquarius. Based on astrology, they believe changes will gradually take place between 1984 and 2020 until our planet is aligned with Aquarius.

New Agers offer many alluring promises. On a global scale, they promise world peace; we will all come together as one and live in harmony and peace. This will be based on sharing. This age will be characterized by a world without war, prejudice, or hunger, and with economic prosperity, reduction of taxes, rehabilitation of prisoners, new educational systems, advancements in medicine and business, technological breakthroughs, and interplanetary travel and colonization. All this will come from the positive energy that is released in the world.

New Agers believe in reincarnation, psychic experiences, communication with people from outer space, and channeling. Channeling is the process through which spirits or beings from outer space communicate by temporarily taking over another person's body. Shirley McClain is probably the most recognizable of the New Agers and has sold eight million copies of her books on the topic. One of her books, *Out on a Limb*, was made into a television movie. Other prominent New Age devotees come from the entertainment industry, including Richard Gere, Sting, Tina Turner, Oprah Winfrey, and Sharon Gless. Bookstores devoted to New Age materials have been in existence for years, but the growing interest in the New Age has now caught the attention of major booksellers. B. Daltons reserves space for a selection from among 5,000 titles on holistic health, wellness and medicine, and other New Age topics. Where once people had to seek out information on the New Age, today it is readily available on our TVs and in our bookstores.

7

Rock Music. The content of the music our children listen to is often disturbing. A typical example of such music comes from the popular rock star Prince, who sold ten million copies of his album *Purple Rain.* One song on the album titled "Darling Nikki" includes these lyrics: "I knew a girl named Nikki/Guess [you] could say she was a sex fiend/I met her in a hotel lobby/Masturbating with a magazine." In the song "Violent Love" by Ted Nugent teenagers hear "Took her in the room with the mirrors on the walls,/Showed her my brand new whip . . . /Screamed as she started to slip/Give me a dose/Of your violent love."

The spiritual implications of the activities of some prominent personalities in rock music are troubling. One album cover of the popular rock group Black Sabbath featured the cross of Christ upside down. A later album cover, *Sabbath Bloody Sabbath*, showed a nude satanic ritual. The numbers 666 were stamped across the front. Ozzie Osbourne, the original lead singer of the group, is notorious for biting off the head of a live bat while performing on stage. Replacement lead singer, Ronnie James Dio, once encouraged fans to salute the devil as a cross burst into flame on stage.

Pornography. After serving on a federal governmental committee to investigate the pornography problem, Dr. James Dobson participated in producing the film *A Winnable War.* As indicated in this excellent but disturbing film, pornography shown in magazines, books, movies, and videos now depicts more than just a sex act between an adult female and male. Some portray urination and defecation, bestiality, and even death. Women are often made up to look like small children and presented in easily obtained pornographic publications. While the government committee was distressed at the content of the pornography it saw, it was also concerned over the proliferation and growing distribution system of that industry. No longer does one have to visit an adult bookstore or movie theater to view pornography. It is now convenient and "safe" to watch these things in secret in one's own home via videocassette or cable TV.

Television. Television has been under attack for the last two decades for its violence and promotion of sexual immorality. Many popular shows would be without plots if sexual

8

innuendo and violence were eliminated. The content of TV shows is of particular concern because of the exposure children and adults have to the medium and its potential effect on them. One study confirmed that some preschoolers watch as much as eighty-eight hours per week and by the time they graduate from high school, they will have spent 22,000 hours watching TV—twice as much time as that spent in school.

Occultism. Occult refers to that which is hidden, mysterious, or beyond human understanding. As the proliferation of the New Age Movement and belief in parapsychological phenomenon such as ESP demonstrate, interest in the occult is on the rise in America. Nationally distributed tabloids routinely publish predictions for future events, horoscopes are printed in most newspapers around the country, and a few well-known celebrities consult mediums and astrologers about important decisions. These applications of the occult seem dangerous enough, but some have gone so far as to explain mystical experiences by attributing the event to the work of demons or Satan. Some even worship Satan and attempt to practice witchcraft.

Reports of occult practices come from citizens and law enforcement agencies. While some occult acts are done in secret, others have high visibility. Startling eyewitness accounts of satanic worship give testimony to the problem. Reports from police investigators describe animal and human sacrifices, including one account of a victim forced to drink his own blood before dying. One cult expert estimates that occult incidents, primarily animal slaughter and mutilation, have increased by fifty percent over the past five years.

Secular Humanism. Humanism refers to the belief in the dignity of humans and the need for humans to reach their full potential. Some humanists, sometimes called secular humanists, deliberately avoid considering God in their emphasis on human potential. The influence of secular humanism is another prominent concern of Christians. The battle over teaching evolution but not creation in our schools, the expunging of our religious heritage from textbooks, the explosion of pornographic books and movies, and even the banning of public nativity scenes at Christmas are all seen as evidence of secular humanism at work. Many Christians are familiar with the

9

work of Madeline O'Hare, who spent years attempting to remove Christian symbols from our schools and culture.

Surveying even a short list of the frontal attacks on Christian beliefs can easily convince one that elements of society are promoting lifestyles antithetical to the Christian life. It is reasonable for Christians to feel their beliefs are under attack from those outside the faith and right for them to be concerned about this frontal assault on their values. Throughout the New Testament from the words of Jesus Christ, Paul, and James we are told to expect trouble (John 15:18-20; James 1:2-12). As Christians, we need to be aware of these influences and prepared to respond. But in recent years, drawing the battle lines has become more difficult because the attacks appear to be coming not only from the front but also from the rear.

Attack from the Rear

Many people within the Christian community are responding with zeal to the cultural dangers surrounding Christians and sounding loud alarms. The cover of one popular book reports, "Today Christians are being deceived by a new worldview more subtle and more seductive than anything the world has ever experienced."[2] The cover of another best-seller reads, "Most people today do not realize what humanism really is and how it is destroying our culture, families, country—and one day, the entire world."[3] An author on the New Age Movement states, "It appears to culminate in a scheme both fulfilling the prophetic requirements for the Antichrist as set forth in the Bible, and also matching Nazism down to use of swastikas."[4]

After reading a number of these books with conspiracy theories and apocalyptic themes, one begins to get a sense of unreality—a feeling that legitimate concern has been overstated. Christians can overuse emotional appeals just as our opponents do. This rear attack on some parts of our belief system has opened up, like a civil war, from within the Christian ranks.

By using a bag of tricks that contain logical fallacies, mind tricks, exaggerations, bad reasoning, and partial knowledge, some Christians have damaged their credibility. In some cases, they have not only damaged their own credibility but the credibility of Christians at large.

In September of 1988 there were Christians who were expecting the Rapture — that is, the removal of the church from the world by Christ — to occur because of what they had read in the booklet by Edgar Whisenant *On Borrowed Time*.[5] Whisenant outlined eighty-eight reasons the Lord would return in 1988. For the few months leading up to the "calculated" date, the booklet sold at a frenzied pace in Christian bookstores all over North America. For a short while it was a hot topic of debate, curiosity, criticism, and finally dismissal among Christians. The "eighty-eight reasons mania" was covered by local and national news media across the country. A few quit their jobs and kept their children from school in anticipation. When the predicted event failed to happen, not only did the author of the booklet and those who followed him and his teachings look foolish, Christians everywhere were somewhat discredited in the eyes of many non-Christians. Looking foolish for truth, as Christian leaders have done for centuries, is admirable, but looking foolish for untruth harms the Christian cause.

While God has supplied the church with teachers, people gifted to explain the Scriptures to other people, He has also given us His Spirit to teach us. We are not to receive blindly whatever is taught in the church. It is the Christian's duty to verify it against the Scriptures like the Bereans did in the early church (Acts 17:11). Had this been done with the teaching received from *On Borrowed Time*, many would not have been led astray.

Unfortunately, those outside the Christian faith gain most of their exposure to Christianity by observing the events that come to public attention. As they observe fallen television evangelists and failed predictions of the rapture, they often form impressions of Christians as those who are unable to think critically. Many critics of Christianity including Celsus, Bertrand Russell, Alan Watts, and Albert Ellis have observed that Christians don't know how to think well. Those who fail to base their points on sound reason and Scripture often end up repelling those who might otherwise be interested in our faith. Consider a few examples.

Satanic Messages. Most of us have heard of backmasking and subliminal messages in recorded rock music. The debate continues over whether or not either practice is being done or having an effect. Al Menconi, a noted authority on all forms of rock music who also happens to be a Christian, is certain that backmasking is a fabrication of some people's imagination. There are others who suggest that a few songs, such as Led Zeppelin's "Stairway to Heaven," contain backward messages with occult implications. But legitimate warnings can degenerate through faulty logic, lack of information, and uncritical thinking into witch-hunts. According to evangelists Jim Brown and Gregg Hudson, there is a satanic message recorded backward in the theme song of *Mr. Ed*, a popular television show in the 1950s (and now in reruns) about a talking horse. The two evangelists argue that listeners can hear, when the music is played backward, "Someone sung the song for Satan," and that this is designed to influence the listener. Controlled research by John Vokey and Don Read of the University of Lethbridge indicates that most backward messages were not deliberately recorded but are a result of active construction on the part of the listener. Moreover, Vokey and Read demonstrated that backward or subliminal messages appear to be completely ineffective in influencing attitudes or changing behaviors.

Rock Music. In addition to the concern about backmasked subliminal messages, Christians have attributed a number of other evils to rock music. Rock music is seen by some to be a way of opening our culture to communism. David Noebel, author of *The Marxist Minstrels*, writes, "The Communist infiltration into the subversion of American music has been nothing short of phenomenal and in some areas, e.g., folk music, their control is fast approaching the saturation point . . . ."[6]

The New Age Movement. Many are interested in New Age topics, but the presence of competing religions does not imply a conspiracy. Constance Cumbey, an attorney and author on the New Age Movement, uses the words "conspirators," "code words," and "infiltrators," when discussing the movement. In *The Hidden Dangers of the Rainbow*, Cumbey writes that the reason New Agers put small rainbow decals on their automobiles and bookstores is to signal to others in the movement. Cumbey also writes, "By networking they have

12

achieved a synergetic effect that makes them nearly unstoppable."[7] Cumbey even ties the New Age Movement with efforts to bring the Antichrist to earth.

Satanic Toys and Cartoons. According to Phil Phillips, author of *Turmoil in the Toybox,* cartoons as seemingly innocent as the Smurfs are laden with the occult. Phillips also identifies the *My Little Pony* cartoons and toys as satanic. Phillips writes, "Because these toys are based on mythological creatures, they are occult . . . ."[8] What about the cute and cuddly Care Bears? The Care Bears have been described as tainted with humanism, magic, and Eastern religions. And Rainbow Brite? The use of the rainbow tips one off to "Rainbow Brite" since to New Agers the rainbow signifies the bridge (antahkarana) between Lucifer and man.

Television. Televison certainly plays a prominent role in the lives of children and adults today. But is it as harmful as some Christian critics make it sound? Phillips goes so far as to suggest that television is harmful because electrodes in the brain react by releasing a depressant. Thus, he concludes, the brain reacts as it would to an addictive depressant medication.

Secular Humanism. Secular humanism is difficult to define but continues to be a concern of Christians. According to Tim LaHaye, author of *The Battle for the Mind,* ". . . the humanists want to control the lives and destinies of the world's peoples, and they intend their takeover by the twenty-first century."[9] LaHaye also writes, ". . . at this time of destiny, the church is sound asleep, and unless . . . Christians wake up to who the enemy really is, the humanists will accomplish their goal of a complete world takeover by the year 2000."[10]

Psychological Seduction. Many Christians have been critical of the influence psychology is having on the church. One Christian critic, William Kilpatrick, argues that psychology is not only ineffective for treating psychological disorders, it may also be causing them. To support this assertion he observes that increases in suicide rates have been accompanied by increases in suicide prevention centers. Although cautious in how he interprets this finding, Kilpatrick hints at the possibility that psychology has created and perpetuated emotional problems.[11] Dave Hunt and T. A. McMahon, popular Christian authors, have noted a cover-up within psychology. They believe psychologists have conspired to deliberately keep vital information from the public to protect their self-interest. Things are so bad that Hunt and McMahon write, "The damning truth has been (and still is) systematically covered up in what amounts to an international scandal unparalleled in history."[12] Evangelist Jimmy Swaggart has suggested that marriage counseling is leading many of America's young pastors into sexual immorality.[13]

Are Christians Becoming Paranoid?

Paranoia is the unjustified belief that others are intending harm. Those diagnosed as paranoid believe they have discovered secret knowledge, or that they have been able to see connections between events that others have missed. It is this secret knowledge, special insight, or ability to connect unassociated events that allows them to see the conspiracy others have overlooked. Conspiracy theories usually build around bits and pieces of facts that are verifiable and true in their context, but the paranoid mind assembles these facts together with imaginative leaps of logic and produces erroneous conclusions. Examining the extreme positions and claims of some Christian spokespeople suggests a kind of paranoia.

Yes, extreme humanism is sometimes a threat to the beliefs of Christians, but is it really part of a plot to control the world by the year 2000? Yes, the New Age Movement seems to be popular, but is it part of a plot to bring the Antichrist to earth? Do all those with rainbows in their windows belong to this conspiracy? (We hope not. One of our daughters has a rainbow in her window. She made it from a kit bought with money she saved from her allowance.) Yes, some rock music has disgusting content (shock rock), but is it part of a communist conspiracy? Yes, there are more divorces and more counselors than in the past, and there are those who receive marriage counseling and finally file for divorce. But is it surprising that some people who come to marriage counselors end up divorced? Is it also suspicious that some people who go to hospitals die, or that some people who visit auto mechanics end up stranded on the highway? Backmasked satanic messages in rock music? In the *Mr. Ed* theme song? Smurfs a satanic toy? Psychology involved in a cover-up scandal "unparalleled in history"?

Surviving the Crossfire

Whether it be a frontal attack from the enemy or a rear attack from our own troops, both sides in the war for our hearts and minds will perceive and reshape truth to support their perspectives. Sometimes the attacks will use exaggeration and conspiracy theories. But when these theories and charges are carefully examined, their "proof" unravels into pieces of unrelated facts. It is then we can say the conspiracy theorists were either uninformed, misinformed, or illogical. The key to surviving both sets of attacks is to become Christian critical thinkers.

Most of us are already committed to using our minds in Bible study and in reading books and articles that help our Christian walk. But we also need to commit ourselves to a self-defense program allowing us to resist the persuasive forces of the information age. Part of this defense program should be the development of a strategy, a plan of defense and attack, that can be used when confronted with extreme ideas. How can we best respond to the informational crossfire in which we live? Throughout this book we address this question by exploring principles of critical thinking and issues of specific importance to Christians. As an introduction to the rest of the book, consider the following five suggestions for Christian critical thinking.

1. *Compare claims with Scripture.* The Christian critical **15** thinker needs a working knowledge of Scripture for a defense. It is easy to proof-text opinions by quoting verses out of context. The thinking Christian needs to know how to read and interpret the Bible. In his book, *Beyond Seduction,* Dave Hunt warns, "We must be careful not to approach the Bible with our own prior opinions in an attempt to find verses that we can somehow use to justify what we already want to believe."[14] This is excellent advice, but the use Hunt makes of Scripture in the book has been questioned by many as a proof-text approach. He argues against self-esteem, for example, based on Paul's warning to Timothy that in the last times there will be

"lovers of self." Does this mean Christians must dislike themselves in order to be adequately spiritual?

The themes of forgiveness, love, correction, and self-discipline are woven together throughout Scripture. Contradictory apocalyptic messages, harsh attacks on fellow Christians, and claims of special knowledge or insight may be warning signs of Scripture being misused.

2. *Compare claims with life experience.* There is no reason to believe one person's experiences are better or more accurate than another's. So there is no reason to discount one's own perceptions in favor of another's. Take for example the claims about the amount of time teenagers watch TV and listen to rock music. Based on the figures given by some critics, the average child would be spending up to ten hours a day in these activities. If we assume teens sleep eight hours a night and spend at least six hours a day in school, we have accounted for the twenty-four hours in a typical day. But what about talking on the phone; isn't that a major teen activity? What about sports, parties, socializing, dating, hanging around, part-time jobs, travel to and from school and jobs, homework, church, youth groups, and a host of other activities that take up the time of teenagers?

The same questions can be asked about younger children. The statistics regarding exposure to television given earlier require a child to watch television four to six hours a day. But what about play, mealtimes, travel to and from school, Boy Scouts, Girl Scouts, Awanas, Indian Guides, swimming lessons, dance lessons, acrobatics, gymnastics, and all the other activities that make mothers and fathers feel like chauffeurs? It may be that children and teens are watching TV and listening to rock music while doing these other activities, but it seems more reasonable to question the statistics given. Maybe children don't watch as much television and listen to as much rock music as some would have us believe. There are valid reasons to be concerned about TV and rock music, but the concerns need to balanced with sound reason.

3. *Compare claims with logic.* One of the easiest ways to test the validity of an idea is to test its logic. If someone speaks for God then the message should be logical and reasonable. For example, there probably have been backmasked messages in

16

rock music. But what about the claim of messages in the *Mr. Ed* theme song? The song for the show was written before backmasking became a popular idea. One study on backmasking showed that people do indeed hear messages when songs are played backward, but *only* if they are first told what to hear. Would a true persuasive message be dependent on knowing what to hear?

Another example of weak logic can be found in the claim by Hunt and McMahon that psychology is trying to hide its ineffectiveness. The results of the ineffective Cambridge-Somerville youth project, which they refer to as a skeleton in psychology's closet, were published in *American Psychologist*, the journal of the American Psychological Association that is sent to every member of the APA. The study Hunt and McMahon claim was suppressed was conducted by psychologists, written by psychologists, published by the APA, sent to its 50,000 members, and is available in virtually every college and university library in the country. Wouldn't it have been easier to suppress the damning evidence by not publishing it?

4. *Avoid overgeneralization.* Overgeneralization is the tendency to believe what is true in one situation must be true in all situations. An example of this is some of what we hear about rock music. There is a vast range of rock music and most of it is not shock rock. It is true that much of the content describes a lifestyle that Christians would not want to model, but there is Christian rock, and, like in most industries, there are Christians in rock.

Another kind of overgeneralization is assuming that everyone will have similar responses to events. If rock music led one person to ruin then it will lead all to ruin. But what about individual differences? Are all people influenced identically, or do some respond differently? Thousands of psychological studies demonstrate that not all individuals respond in the same way. In the playground at a nearby elementary school, children climbed on a jungle gym for years without a mishap. One day a child fell and suffered a concussion. The next week the jungle gym was removed. It may have been a needless overgeneralization. We need to be cautious not to build rules on exceptions.

17

5. *Read several perspectives.* Whether reading Christian or secular authors, it is a good practice to look for another source on the same topic. Scripture teaches us that people are infinitely fallible. As much as we would like to believe that others are less fallible than ourselves, it just isn't so. In checking multiple sources, we often find contradictions. For example, in Constance Cumbey's book *The Hidden Dangers of the Rainbow*, Cumbey makes it clear that there is a conspiracy on the part of those involved in the New Age Movement. Cumbey alleges that "network" and "synergy" are magic words for New Agers. "By networking they have achieved a synergetic effect that makes them nearly unstoppable."[15] But Douglas Groothius, another Christian expert on the New Age Movement, disagrees with Cumbey's conspiracy theory. Groothius notes that every New Age group is not consciously trying to take over the world and that conspiracy theories lack concrete evidence. "Showing connections between people and groups is one thing; showing conspiracy is another."[16] Two authors, both Christian, have different perspectives.

The difficult task for Christians is walking the thin line between legitimate concern and paranoia. If Christians step too far to one side they are pulled into a world of secular extremists and away from their faith in God. If Christians step too far to the other side they are sucked into the strange world of Christian extremists. As Christians walk this line they are pulled from both sides in an ideological tug-of-war — a tug-of-war in which both sides are well prepared for the struggle to persuade. Christian critical thinking is the stabilizing influence we need to survive the information age.

CHAPTER TWO

Do Christians Have a Corner on Truth?

The heavens declare the glory of God; the skies proclaim the work of his hands. Psalm 19:1

In the seventeenth century Galileo Galilei pointed his telescope at the sky and concluded Copernicus had been right—the sun was the center of the solar system. He published his radical theory in 1610, and his book was soon placed on the Vatican's *Index of Prohibited Books.* Galileo was found guilty of teaching doctrine that was "absurd, false in philosophy and formally heretical . . . that can in no way be probable, which has been already declared and finally determined contrary to the Divine Scripture."[1]

In this case the prevailing religious leaders didn't have a corner on truth. In our age of space exploration and astrophysics, it seems ridiculous to view the earth as the center of the universe. But church leaders in Galileo's time had some persuasive evidence from which they justified such a conclusion. God had labored five days to create the earth but only one day to create the rest of the universe. Clearly the earth was a special place, favored by God, in the center of the universe. When Joshua needed more daylight to conquer the Amorites, he asked God to stop the sun in the sky, and "the sun stood still." (Joshua 10:13) This request was in accordance with Joshua's view of the world. And his report, "And the sun stood still," was also consistent with that perspective. He was unaware that the earth he stood on was rotating on an axis, circling the sun, and part of a galaxy moving through the universe. His description and conclusion in this passage were based on his observation or experience.

What was the error that leaders of the Catholic Church made in holding Galileo to a geocentric view of the universe? It was primarily an error of misinterpreting the intent of a Bible passage. This story of Joshua is a rich narrative illustrating God's redemptive nature. It is a story about what God did to and through people and shows that He is the hero. The purpose of this narrative is not to provide us with a clue as to the mechanics of the motion of the earth. Nor is it a definitive account of how an omnipotent God physically lengthened the time between sunrise and sunset.

The error made by the church leaders flowed from an unreasonably strong desire to provide an explanation. They read their perspective of the world into this story, coupled this evidence with their theological view, and charged Galileo as a heretic when his scientific observations conflicted with church dogma.

Similarly, we can fall prey to such fallacies today. There's a flash in the sky that catches our eye. We look for a plane. We strain to see it, but it is gone. Our curiosity causes us to read about "unexplainable sightings in the sky." We begin to develop conclusions — all based on speculation. Even our speculation may be based upon previous speculation. Finally, our pseudoscientific story is found without basis and farfetched. We are then discredited.

Galileo was eventually vindicated, but he did not live to see the church change its position, reevaluate Scripture, and come to a better understanding of both God's Word and God's world. Despite sincere conviction, the religious leaders of Galileo's day were wrong.

20

In 1690 a woman living in Edinburgh was burned at the stake by the order of King James VI because she used an anesthetic during childbirth to help relieve the pain. Anesthesia for labor pain was considered heretical by the theologians of the day since the Scripture clearly states, "With pain you will give birth to children." (Genesis 3:16) Today we don't burn women at the stake, nor do we require them to suffer during childbirth to pay for Eve's sin. Some scholars believe that the word that was translated "pain" could also be translated as "work." Childbirth is a lot of work with or without anesthetics. In this case, what was practiced by the church in 1690 is no longer practiced today. Have we strayed from truth or are we closer to it? In the dark days of slavery, many slave owners condoned their practices with Scripture (1 Timothy 6:1, 2). Others have used Scripture to support witch burning (Exodus 22:18). The textbook of the Inquisition, *Malleus Maleficarum* (Hammer of the Witches), included a detailed section on methods of examining witches guaranteed to obtain confessions. The book was written by two Dominican priests and endorsed by the faculty of theology of the University of Cologne in 1487. It is estimated that 200,000 to 500,000 witches were executed after being tortured into confessions. Eighty-five percent of those executed were women. While these activities were happening, the church clung tenaciously to the great commandments to love (Matthew 19:19) and to show mercy (Matthew 5:7).

Today we don't believe in slavery, burning witches, or an earth-centered universe. But at various periods in the history of the Christian church, each was accepted with supposedly biblical justification. Does biblical truth change with time? Certainly not. What was thought to be infallible scriptural truth was actually fallible human interpretation of Scripture. It's humbling to respect history, realizing that some of what we accept as truth today will be recognized as false in centuries to come.

The problems of inaccurate interpretation are not limited to theology. Science is filled with examples of misinterpreting data. Newtonian physics was accepted as "truth" until Einstein found contradictory evidence. Just as Einsteinian physics became known as "truth," researchers began finding data that fit better with quantum physics. 21

Because scientists recognize the tentative nature of "truth," they use theories and hypotheses. Because theologians recognize the tentative nature of "truth," they employ hermeneutics and apologetics. In science the goal is to understand God's world; in theology it is to know God, His works, and His relationship to humans. These two disciplines are not always separate and unrelated as they address subjects.

In Galileo's time, Scripture was interpreted according to the church's understanding of the world. Science, however, was beginning to arrive at different conclusions based upon physical observations. Eventually the church accepted Galileo's position and came to a new understanding of Scripture. This interplay between God's Word, God's world, and human reasoning reminds us of our human limitations.

Knowing God

God reveals Himself in two ways. First, He reveals Himself to us through the Bible, a special revelation. Second, God is known through His created order, a general revelation. The psalmist says, "The heavens are telling the glory of God." (Psalm 19:1) Paul refers to general revelation when he speaks of God as being known through creation (Romans 1:20). General revelation is available to all people and all nations.

Some Christians object to the idea we can understand or construct a knowledge of God by observing the world. Martin and Deidre Bobgan write, "Perhaps they think that what has been observed in nature by the limited minds of men equals God's truth. The Bible contains the only pure truth of God. All else is distorted by the limitations of human perception."[2]

General revelation can be misinterpreted. For example, Nazi theologians claimed knowledge of God and His will through general revelation. They argued that the natural order in God's creation (with German superiority) justified the existence of a Nazi state.

What the Bobgans fail to realize is that Scripture, God's special revelation, is also open to misinterpretation. Nazis considered the special revelation of the Old and New Testaments to be a "Jewish swindle."[3] They misinterpreted Scripture because they went looking for support for a theological position they had already established. Many psychological studies have shown we are good at finding what we look for because of our preconceptions. (This will be discussed in more detail in Chapter 3.)

Dave Hunt warns about this danger in his book *Beyond Seduction: A Return to Biblical Christianity.* Hunt writes:

> We must be careful not to approach the Bible with our own prior opinions in an attempt to find verses that we can somehow use to justify what we already want to believe. Succumbing to this temptation has probably brought more

problems into the church than anything else. On the contrary we must let the Bible teach and change us.[4]

Yet Hunt's books are critical of some of the most prominent Christian leaders, most of whom claim their views are biblical. Different scholars interpret Scripture differently. It seems pretentious for anyone to claim he or she has the "pure truth of God" when others look at the same words and come up with different truths. Special revelation and general revelation both require human interpretation, and human interpretation is fallible. As Ted Ward, professor at Trinity Evangelical Divinity School, has said, "In the realm of ideas the tendency to draw lines can become a barrier to truth."

Galileo's trial, the burning of women who used anesthesia, the Spanish Inquisition, the Crusades, and the proliferation of Christian denominations provide strong evidence that Scripture can be interpreted and misinterpreted in a variety of ways. Even when one is a sincere Christian who reads, believes, and desires to obey the Bible, mistakes can still be made in interpreting and applying the Scriptures.

As imperfect as it is, reasoning is our greatest tool in understanding God's revelations. God inspired Scripture with the intent that we could understand and apply it. The New Testament contains letters to the early churches, written by the apostles, that address problems and provide ways of interpreting and applying the words of Christ and the Jewish Scriptures. But as we use our reasoning to interpret Scripture, it is important to humbly acknowledge our human limits and inclination to be overconfident in whatever interpretation we believe is correct. Every passage of Scripture and every discovery and theory about God's world must be detected, perceived, processed, interpreted (in terms of previous knowledge and experience), and expressed. In this complicated process, some truth is discovered, and some fallacy, like that of an earth-centered universe, is perpetuated.

Is All Truth God's Truth?

While it seems unreasonable to reject all general revelation, it is reasonable to be concerned with how general and special revelation relate. There are limits to general revelation.

Studying the world will not reveal God's plan for salvation. There are also limits to special revelation. The Bible tells us to feed the hungry but doesn't tell us the most efficient way to farm or distribute food. While it instructs us about business ethics, the Bible is not a textbook on agribusiness.

The search for God's truth is complicated further by the observation that God doesn't require truth to come through His Word or His people. A discovery by an atheist physicist is just as true as a discovery by a Christian physicist. A development in third-world food distribution might initially be made by an agnostic and later used by committed Christians for God's glory.

God's world and God's Word cannot contradict each other. Whether a Christian or an atheist discovers some scientific or historical truth, it is still God's truth because He caused all truth. Ultimately, if science continues to move toward truth and if Scripture is interpreted correctly, there will be no conflict between general and special revelation. For example, few Christians today believe that prayer alone is sufficient treatment for physical illness. Most will seek the help of a doctor *and* pray for recovery. This illustrates a healthy appreciation for God's world (partially discovered in medical science) and God's Word.

A Corner on Truth?

One unfortunate theme in the writings of Christian extremists is a selective acceptance of general revelation. Authors who would presumably go to a physician for antibiotics argue that going for counseling is somehow anti-Christian. Dave Hunt argues that Scripture is sufficient for human needs and that psychology is harmful, stating:

> The Bible is filled with examples of men and women, young and old, who suffered traumas and trials such as many of those now seeking psychological help have never even imagined.... It is an insult to God and His Word to say that help is now needed from another source, particularly when the lives of those who conceived these humanistic theories pale beside the shining heroes and heroines of the faith.[5]

Such a perspective ignores individual differences and assumes that everyone is capable of responding the way Bible heroes did. It also assumes Bible characters didn't seek help from those qualified to help. And this perspective ignores those in Scripture who repeatedly failed to live up to expectations and were corrected or punished by God, including Adam, Eve, Cain, Moses, Jonah, and Saul.

Hunt and other extremists may never need to see a psychologist, but when they dismiss an entire academic discipline they claim a corner on truth. Although many Christians will never seek psychological treatment, others will. And, according to studies of the results of psychotherapy, most of those who seek help will benefit. A college professor used to chide his students and other faculty for wasting so much of their lives sleeping. The professor repeatedly bragged that he slept only four to five hours a night and that this was more than sufficient. It was clear the professor regarded those who slept more as weak and in need of more self-discipline. But people vary in the amount of sleep they need—some need more than others. To assume otherwise is to be insensitive to individual differences and is ultimately egocentric.

Extremists often go to unreasonable lengths to support or protect their beliefs. Throughout the Old and New Testaments they used intrigue, violence, force, and deception to carry out their ends. One of the apostles, Simon, was from a Jewish political party known as the Zealots—a militant, patriotic group, willing to kill another Israelite out of zeal for Jewish law. Today the war has de-escalated to one of ideas and words—without the physical violence.

25

Both general and special revelation are gifts from God, but both require human interpretation and careful reasoning. As critical thinkers, we need to be cautious when we hear dogmatic claims that reject parts of general revelation.

Speaking from the Corner

Extremists are usually well-intentioned individuals wanting to purify the kingdom of God. However, their claims require careful scrutiny. By accepting only some general revelation or claiming exclusive insight into God's special revelation, they sometimes arrive at erroneous conclusions. When this is done repeatedly, it causes credibility problems. Several problems are associated with taking extremist positions.

Problem 1: *They sound irrational.* By claiming special access to truth, many extremists have resorted to irrational reasoning. An example can be seen in a discussion of meditation and relaxation. In Richard Foster's *Celebration of Discipline*, he calls Christians to the biblical practices of meditation, fasting, and prayer. Widely read and admired, Foster's book is biblically orthodox. It even stimulated a film series designed to teach the spiritual disciplines. But a few years after its publication, Dave Hunt and T. A. McMahon disagreed with Foster in *The Seduction of Christianity*, claiming a link between Christian meditation and occult sorcery. They admonished believers to stay away from meditation, noting that it comes from basic teachings of occultism. Later, on a television talk show, Hunt explained that relaxation and meditation cause the soul to lose control over the body, allowing evil spirits to come in and take control.

Is it rational to label Christian or biblical meditation an occult practice? Are those who found Richard Foster's instruction useful and spiritually fulfilling unwittingly dabbling in the occult?

Meditation can be used in pagan practices, but there is nothing inherently evil about it. Eastern religions use meditation but they also use prayer. Are we to abandon prayer also? Meditation, prayer, and other Christian disciplines become Christian when they are put to use in accordance with the Scriptures.

The extremists' messages are diverse: The *Mr. Ed* TV show was part of a satanic plot; humanists are plotting to take over the world; New Agers are plotting to end the world; TV executives are part of the plots; government officials are part of the plots; and anyone who does not agree that there are plots is either part of the plot or ignorant. After a while, these conspiracy theories begin to look quite irrational.

Problem 2: *Some extremist claims distract us from the more important issues.* Remember the Beatles tune containing the lyrics "I Wanna Hold Your Hand"? Today rock music advocates holding a lot more than a hand. Christians have good reason to be concerned about the lyrics. But our

26

attention has been distracted by peripheral claims. We may be so concerned with backward lyrics that we forget to notice the greater danger of forward lyrics.

Gary Greenwald, senior pastor of Eagle's Nest Christian Fellowship in Santa Ana, California, travels the country preaching against rock music. He demonstrates the presence of backmasked messages by playing songs by Queen and Jefferson Starship. The backward messages can be perceived in some songs if the audience is first told what they may hear. By giving his audience a "perceptual set," Greenwald actually predisposes his listeners to hear the supposed message. But the messages themselves are usually just random noises caused by backward sound patterns. In one study of backmasking, Vokey and Read played passages of Lewis Carrol's poem, *Jabberwocky*, backward. Remember that this poem was written in 1871, before the invention of the phonograph. When they played the tape for participants, none of them could decipher any messages. After three attempts the participants could still not hear a message. But if the researchers then told the participants to listen for "snatched her nips," the message suddenly leapt off the tape at them. If they told the participants to listen for "I saw a girl with a weasel in her mouth," that message leapt off the tape at them. Even "I saw Satan" could be heard once it was suggested to the participants. The participants were able to make out twelve different messages in two backward passages, but only the messages for which they were told to listen.

One might also wonder whether musicians who deliberately put backward messages on albums can effectively persuade listeners. Pastor Greenwald blames the messages for leading Christians into moral sin. It is tempting to reason that if the messages are there, then they must be effective. But Vokey and Read's research suggests that even when messages are present, they have no effect on the listener.

Attacks from the rear, from within our Christian community, prevent a person from preparing for frontal assaults. By focusing on irrational concerns, we are distracted from more important issues. This can also be seen in the current debate over children's toys.

Are today's toys bad for our children, or are the concerns expressed about toys the result of overactive imaginations? The manufacturers make a good point when they say, "Like any corporation this size, we have plenty of observant and born-again Christians who have input into all our decisions."[6] We tend to forget that Christians are part of corporations that we think of as "secular."

In response to the reaction against certain toys, there are now companies that offer Christian toy alternatives to concerned parents. Instead of action figures such as G.I. Joe, He-Man, and Rambo, parents can buy their children Sampson, Moses, and John the Baptist. Instead of a Darth Vader helmet and light sword, parents can buy their children the full armor of God, which includes the breastplate of righteousness, the shield of faith, the helmet of salvation, and the sword of the Spirit. In the stuffed animal category, the parents can buy Born Again Bunny, Sanctified Skunk, Holy Cow, Heavenly Hound, and Promise Puppy. There is also a full line of stuffed bears including Angel Bear (which has wings), Truthful Teddy, Baby Bear, and Good Deed Bear. The existence of such toys, however, does not automatically end a parent's concern.

Many questions arise from marketing Christian toys. Do children playing with Christian toys play differently from those playing with non-Christian toys, and do they turn out to be more Christian than children from similar backgrounds who play with mainstream toys? Does a boy smacking his little brother over the head with the sword of the Spirit learn anything different than the boy who smacks his brother with a light sword? Does cuddling up to Heavenly Hound do something for a child that cuddling up to a pound puppy doesn't? When a Sampson Action Figure pulls down the temple, crushing his enemies inside, is the child learning anything different from when G.I. Joe blows up the enemy's headquarters? Certainly the Christian toys would be no worse than the secular toys, but is there reason to believe things would be any better?

Arguing over whether children should play with My Little Pony or Rainbow Brite detracts from more significant concerns, such as the influence of violent toys. Extremist claims can distract us from more important issues.

Problem 3: *Extremist claims play into the hands of our critics.* Some critics of Christianity watch us closely. Every

28

time a television evangelist falls they have more evidence that Christianity doesn't work. Extremism sometimes adds fuel to the fire.

The Humanist, a periodical whose title gives a clue as to its worldview, is frequently hostile to Christianity, claiming Christians are ignorant and blind to important issues. It's easy to take offense at this until one is exposed to some of the extremist claims made by Christians against humanism. Each extremist provides more evidence to humanist writers that Christians are naive and poorly informed.

According to Tim LaHaye, secular humanists "control everything—the mass media, government, and even the Supreme Court."[7] Jerry Falwell has been quoted as saying that "Humanism challenges every principle on which America was founded. It advocates abortion on demand, recognition of homosexuals, free use of pornography, legalizing of prostitution and gambling, and free use of drugs, among other things."[8] These warnings of secular humanism are overstated. Rather than identifying with evidence the real dangers of humanism, they have only contributed to the humanists' view that Christians are poorly informed. The fact is that many humanists are as concerned about pornography, drug use, and other social problems as Christians. John Baker, writing in *The Humanist*, sees fundamentalists as

> ...people who are not intellectually inclined, have little training or interest in science or the processes of critical reasoning, easily accept authority associated with simplistic answers, and are quite worried about the hereafter. Inside this core are leaders, some of whom manipulate the entire movement for personal gain.... Believing and not asking questions is basic to most nonintellectual religions....[9]

29

Of course this is also overstated. Most Christians don't fit Baker's definition any better than humanists fit LaHaye's and Falwell's definitions.

Ironically, humanists believe that Christians belong in the same category as the New Agers. To the humanists, Christians are just another group who have turned to an imaginary spirit world to solve their problems instead of focusing their attention on the real world. This turning away from the world is perceived as anti-intellectual. Baker also writes: "The increasing anti-intellectualism and irrational thinking, including the turn to mysticism, the occult, and the uncritical acceptance of dogma seen in contemporary America, is a typical response of a people who no longer control their own destiny . . ."[10]

By creating extreme arguments—arguments built on faulty logic—both humanists and Christians have strayed from the truth. In the process, we have weakened our position and given our critics grounds for additional criticism. If we have attempted to win the battle with extreme arguments—arguments that employ overgeneralization, name-calling, misrepresentation, or a myriad of other faulty logic tricks—we have committed a moral error. And this moral error is most reprehensible because it has been committed while we were fighting for truth.

Part of the problem comes when an extremist claims to have *the* biblical or Christian view on an issue. *The Christian World View of Psychology and Counseling* and *The Biblical View of Self-Esteem, Self-Love, Self-Image*, two books from Christian authors, imply that there is only one view on these subjects among Christians, that everything is settled, and there is nothing more to be discussed. Actually, many others have differing perspectives on self-esteem and counseling, and they support their differing views with Scripture. Our critics see titles like these and assume there is a single Christian worldview. They, like some zealous authors, fail to understand that there is no one *biblical* or *Christian* view because the Bible requires interpretation, and interpretation requires human reason.

When Christians claim communist agents are behind the lyrics in rock music, people tend to overgeneralize and stop listening to other legitimate Christian concerns. Claiming there is a humanist plot to force pornography onto our children means fewer people will listen to our legitimate concerns about what is taught in school. Extreme positions make it harder to reach the unsaved because they have only seen a parody of the Gospel and the Christian life.

Life in the Crossfire: Making the Best of the Battle ———
Finding truth on the battlefield of ideas is like trying to eat lunch in the middle of a food fight. If we keep our heads down and avoid getting involved in the fight, we can get some free food as it flies by. Sure it's messy, but at least we get a free lunch. Searching for truth in the midst of extreme claims takes similar discipline and often yields important "food for thought."

Critical thinking in the midst of the crossfire of ideas has the advantage of allowing us to seek truth in whatever form it may come. Critical thinkers can find truth in general revelation and in special revelation. Critical thinking stimulates integration of God's world and God's Word.

The debate over psychology illustrates the value of critical thinking and the problems with extreme thinking. Extremism in the psychology-Christianity debate started with psychologists. Sigmund Freud, the father of modern psychology, viewed God as an imaginary transference of a father complex. That is, he believed we invent a God because of unresolved feelings about our own fathers. John Watson, leading American behaviorist, was an outspoken atheist. Albert Ellis, a contemporary theorist and psychotherapist, believes religion makes people emotionally sick. These and other outspoken extremists have created an unnecessary wedge between psychology and Christianity.

Christians have fought back on the front between Christianity and psychology and other fronts such as theology, education, art, music—wherever they have felt threatened. Most recently, Martin and Deidre Bobgan have argued that psychology is unscientific and proven to be ineffective. They state, "...to even hint that the...discoveries of such unredeemed men as Freud, Jung, Rogers, etc. are God's truth is to undermine the very Word of God."[11] They label psychology "psychoheresy." In *America: The Sorcerer's New Apprentice*, Dave Hunt and T. A. McMahon write, "The methods being practiced on the public are of dubious value at best, are harmful at worst, and are based upon contradictory and changing theories for which there is no proof."[12] A publication of the Psychology and Counseling Committee of the Coalition on Revival

31

states that "integration of secular psychology with biblical revelation violates the doctrines of the inerrancy, infallibility, and sufficiency of the Bible."[13]

Despite excesses on both sides, psychology has been a tool to discover some of God's general revelation. Psychology has advanced our knowledge of perception, learning, physiology, education, and memory. It has filled a need with the creation of psychometric tests, including aptitude and achievement tests. In its applied forms it has impacted education, business, and mental health. Clinical psychology has been useful in helping those with marital distress, diagnosing and teaching children with learning disabilities, relieving depression and anxiety, teaching learning strategies to the brain-damaged, and helping those with troubled pasts.

Psychology has become controversial partly because of its success. In recent years many pastors have sought training in psychological counseling skills, and many churches have established counseling centers. The effort to integrate psychology and theology has been so widespread that over a decade ago *The Journal of Psychology and Theology* was created by godly people, trained in evangelistic schools and seminaries, to serve as an exchange of ideas and news. It contains articles that discuss how psychotherapy and Christian theology can be used effectively by and for Christians.

While most Christians are embracing truth discovered in psychology, psychologists seem to be more open to religious worldviews. The American Psychological Association has approved two seminaries for doctoral programs in psychology. The APA now has a division for psychologists interested in religious issues, and evangelical Christians have had leadership roles in the division. Distinguished psychology journals frequently include articles about better understanding clients' religious perspectives.

Christianity and psychology benefit from one another. Those with critical thinking skills are able to pull truth from psychology and truth from Christian theology. As a result, thousands of people are helped each year by pastoral counselors or Christian psychotherapists. Despite the war of extremism, there is a broad middle ground where healing and growth and discovery occur.

The Mine Field of Mediocrity ──────────────

Jesus told His followers not to be of this world (John 15:19), but rather to follow Him. Some will be concerned that looking for the middle ground between extremes is a call to compromise. It is important not to equate extremist views with commitment or devotion. The Pharisees were the extremists of Jesus' day. He did not equate their zeal with true spirituality. Despite their respect and status in the community, Jesus confronted the Pharisees about their divisive ways and lack of compassion.

All around us there are seductive forces and dangers. But there are also dangers of being led astray by those in the faith. Paul warns:

> But I am afraid that just as Eve was deceived by the serpent's cunning, your minds may somehow be led astray from your sincere and pure devotion to Christ. (2 Corinthians 11:3)
>
> For such men are false apostles, deceitful workmen, masquerading as apostles of Christ. And no wonder, for Satan himself masquerades as an angel of light. It is not surprising, then, if his servants masquerade as servants of righteousness. Their end will be what their actions deserve. (2 Corinthians 11:13-15)

Certainly not many of today's extremists are Satan's agents, but Paul's warning points out the need to evaluate all teaching critically, even teaching from within the church. We have an obligation to listen to our brothers and sisters and an obligation to critically evaluate what they say.

33

In writing to the church at Rome, Paul responded to a controversy similar to the ones we see today. The new church was being divided because of arguments over what is proper Christian behavior. Extremists were trying to push their beliefs onto others. Paul writes, "Accept him whose faith is weak, without passing judgment on disputable matters." (Romans 14:1) There are two messages here. First, we are to accept one another regardless of disagreements. Second, there will always be "disputable matters." Paul then goes on to argue moderation and tolerance: "Who are you to judge someone else's servant? To his own master he stands or falls." (Romans 14:4) We need to remember our Master, obey God's guidance, and remain firmly committed to scriptural values. As the above examples demonstrate, extremism does not equal commitment.

Three hundred and fifty years after the trial of Galileo, Pope John Paul II issued a pardon. The conflict between the church and science that had followed Galileo's trial had been unnecessary and painful. Pope John Paul II, speaking before the Vatican's Pontifical Academy of Science, said that he hoped "theologians, scholars and historians . . . might examine more deeply the Galileo case and in an honest recognition of wrongs on whatever side they occur, might make disappear the obstacles that this affair still sets up, in many minds, to a fruitful concord between science and faith, between church and world."[14]

Avoiding extremism is not retreating from truth but embracing truth in whatever form it comes—from general or special revelation. Seeking truth is courageous, not cowardly.

CHAPTER THREE

Watching For Ambushes

Christians have a high calling. We are called to love God with our minds, actively searching for His truth in the midst of those who desire to captivate us with eloquent words, clever arguments, and slick media. Which television evangelists can I believe? To what Christian organization should I send my hard-earned money? Which authors make valid arguments?

Christians need critical thinking skills to help them withstand the ambushes and avoid the pitfalls of the misguided. Understanding persuasion is an important part of developing critical thinking. Vivid anecdotes, illusions of correlation, self-justification, and selective attention can lead to intellectual ambush and result in faulty thinking.

After robbing a gas station and driving the attendant to a remote rural location, Peter Grenier . . . decided to give himself an extra hour of getaway time by simply knocking the attendant out as he had seen it done hundreds of times on TV, leaving nothing more than a lump on the head. . . . When he did so, what he experienced was not the "painless operation" he had witnessed on television, but rather, "a nauseating sound of crushed and mushy flesh as the gun butt smashed into the attendant's head and bore through to a solid bone surface, lubricated by the flow of warm blood."[1]

35

Anecdotes and the Vividness Effect _____

Vivid anecdotes are powerful techniques for persuasion. Concepts can be grasped much more quickly when a concrete, specific example is given. The example above was used to make the point that people often mimic what they see on television. After reading this example, how easily could we watch someone get a prime-time head thumping without recalling this description?

For one concerned about the evils of television, this story is an effective tool in convincing others of the problem. A concrete example not only conveys information but also evokes emotional responses. These kinds of examples are engaging, help focus attention, and are more persuasive than just the presentation of information in a standard format.

Vivid anecdotes can be used for good. Jesus, the master teacher, demonstrated the effectiveness of anecdotes in His use of parables. In Luke 10:25-37 Jesus used an example to explain the commandment, "Love your neighbor as yourself," to a lawyer. "And who is my neighbor?" asked the lawyer. In response Jesus related the parable of the Good Samaritan, making clear the meaning of loving one's neighbor. A third of Jesus' teaching was in parables, testifying to the effectiveness of this technique. The durability of this approach can be seen in the fact that the lessons He taught with parables continue to be effective today.

Examples from life are especially useful in making people aware of their hidden attitudes. The parable of the Good Samaritan made people aware of their prejudices. Good teaching techniques never go out of style. Psychologists Daryl and Sandra Bem use a similar approach to reveal attitudes toward women.[2]

Both my wife and I earned college degrees in our respective disciplines. I turned down a superior job offer in Oregon and accepted a slightly less desirable position in New York where my wife would have more opportunities for part-time work in her specialty. Although I would have preferred to live in a suburb, we purchased a home near my wife's job so that she could have an office at home where she would be when the children returned from school. Because my wife earns a good salary, she can easily afford to pay a housekeeper to do her major household chores. My wife and I share all other tasks around the house equally. For example, she cooks the meals, but I do the laundry for her and help her with many of her other household tasks.

Now read the passage again with the gender reversed.

Both my husband and I earned college degrees in our respective disciplines. I turned down a superior job offer in Oregon and accepted a slightly less desirable position in New York where my husband would have more opportunities for part-time work in his specialty. Although I would have preferred to live in a suburb, we purchased a home near my husband's job so that he could have an office at home where he would be when the children returned from school. Because my husband earns a good salary, he can easily afford to pay a housekeeper to do his major household chores. My husband and I share all other tasks around the house equally. For example, he cooks the meals, but I do the laundry for him and help him with many of his other household tasks.

This sex reversal produces an awareness of our sex role expectations. A brief example like this can communicate more than an entire lecture on sex role perceptions. Similarly, we become more aware of the radical implications of loving our neighbors when we hear the story of the Good Samaritan.

Bringing the Message Home. Vivid examples also help us connect new information with previous experience. If an idea is to be remembered it must somehow be connected to the listener's experience. Again, Jesus' parables did this very well. They focused on everyday places and events. Farmers sowing fields (Mark 4:2-20), workers in vineyards (Matthew 20:1-16), and people at weddings (Matthew 22:1-14) are a few examples. Surely His listeners, familiar with the locations and context, found the parables even more compelling than we do today.

The use of familiar examples helps us connect the point of **37** the speaker with everyday life. For example, Mel and Norma Gabler, authors and critics of public education, tell of a woman who objected to the explicit nature of materials used in a high school sex education class. As a result her son suffered in the classroom.

His teacher was good about walking over to his desk and saying to our six-foot-two football player, "Jim, if your mommy doesn't like what we are studying, why don't you tell her to enroll you in a private school?"[3]

Most of us have been embarrassed in front of a class at one time or another and know how painful it can be. This example effectively brings home the Gablers' point that teachers are not always open to parental input. Phil Phillips, author of *Turmoil in the Toybox*, also uses familiar situations effectively to illustrate how toys and fantasy can displace God in a child's life.

Once my father was ministering at a church and he mentioned my ministry. Briefly he also mentioned He-Man. After the service, a little boy was seen in the parking lot running in circles while holding his He-Man figure in his hand. He kept repeating, "He-Man has more power than Jesus. He-Man has more power than Jesus."

A mother and her young son riding in the car were listening to a sermon on the radio. The minister started to pray, "Our Lord God, the master of the universe . . . ." The little boy jumped up from the back seat of the car and said, "Mommy, God isn't the master of the universe, He-Man is."[4]

These kinds of examples immediately impact consciousness and, especially for parents, strike a believable chord since these are clearly childlike behaviors. While one might disagree with Phillips over how concerned to be with such behaviors, the effectiveness of his examples in bringing his point home cannot be denied. When people see a mass of starving people in Ethiopia on television, they are overwhelmed by the size of the task of providing food. But when their attention is focused on one person or a family, the vividness effect causes them to respond.

Misinformation and the Vividness Effect. Vivid illustrations tend to overwhelm us and capture more than just our imagination. Responding to such illustrations, we often ignore the big picture and focus on the features of a specific case.

We tend to reason from what is available in our memory. Vivid anecdotes and experiences are memorable; that's why they are such a powerful tool for persuasion. Salespeople know the power of vivid experiences and use this to sell products. Test-driving a new car creates an immediate image that tends to overshadow the negative aspects of payments, insurance, gas costs, etc. Walking through a model home makes a similar powerful impression. In one study, by simply getting people to imagine themselves with cable TV, subscription rates increased by twenty-eight percent. Vivid

38

testimonials of lottery winners serve a similar purpose and make winning seem much more likely than it actually is, thus increasing ticket sales. Imagining something makes it seem more imminent and likely to happen. Once something is perceived as likely to happen, we are more willing to pursue that goal.

Unfortunately, anecdotes sometimes cause us to overgeneralize and come to faulty conclusions. Try the following quiz:

Quiz

Which of the following are the more frequent causes of death in the United States?

1. All accidents or strokes?
2. All cancers or heart disease?
3. Botulism or smallpox vaccination?
4. Electrocution or asthma?
5. Homicide or diabetes?
6. Motor vehicle accidents or cancer of the digestive system?
7. Tornado or excess cold?
8. Lightning or appendicitis?
9. Motor vehicle/train collision or tuberculosis?
10. Drowning or leukemia?

The answers are at the end of this chapter. Most people miss the majority of the questions because our judgments are biased by the information we receive. Because we read front-page stories about accidents, electrocution, and cancer, we assume they are common. Vivid examples shape our thinking.

39

Extremists often use anecdotes to make their points. This is not intrinsically wrong (anecdotes are interesting and useful), but authors and readers tend to overgeneralize because of the vividness effect.

In supporting his conclusion that "Nothing is greater than meeting positive people," Robert Schuller gives the following anecdote:

> One summer I was in China and I met a vivacious eighty-three-year-old lady from Arkansas. She was a charming, delightful, positive person. I commented on how enthusiastic she was. "Oh yes, Dr. Schuller," she said. "Ever since

I began watching *Hour of Power,* I've become so positive. You should know that at my age I have four boyfriends." She continued, "I begin my day with 'Will Power,' then I take a walk with 'Arthur Ritis,' come back with 'Charlie Horse,' and I spend my evening with 'Ben Gay.'" Now that's what I call positive thinking![5]

This is a powerful example of a remarkable woman. But critical thinking requires that we be cautious· in generalizing the conclusions. Is it reasonable that other eighty-three-year-olds would have similar results with positive thinking? Will *Hour of Power* always produce this kind of positive thinking? Could her positive thinking be covering up deeper spiritual or emotional needs?

Another example of the misleading nature of vivid examples can be seen in William Kirk Kilpatrick's book *Psychological Seduction.* In the opening to his book, Kilpatrick uses an anecdote from his personal experience to make the point that psychology is replacing religion.

The priest was delivering a sermon, and to buttress his message he referred to the authority of John's Gospel, the Epistles of Saint Paul, the writings of Saint Augustine, and so on. The congregation seemed unmoved. The man to my left yawned. A woman in the next row was checking the contents of her purse. "As Erich Fromm says...," the priest continued. Instantly a visible stir of attention rippled through the crowd as it strained forward to catch every nuance. The yawning man closed his mouth, and the lady shut her purse; both came alert. Erich Fromm.... Of course! If anyone knew the answers to the riddles of life, it would be Erich Fromm.[6]

This kind of experience can easily be overgeneralized and raises some questions. Did anyone else notice the increased attentiveness of the audience? Had the priest ever mentioned Fromm before? Perhaps it was so out of the ordinary that it woke people up. Perhaps Fromm was mentioned for just such a purpose. Even if people did suddenly pay attention, did it necessarily mean that psychology is becoming a new religion?

Another example comes from Constance Cumbey's book, *The Hidden Dangers of the Rainbow.* She relates an incident that helped make her aware of the New Age conspiracy. Having been tipped off to a woman's involvement in the New Age movement because she used the code words "mind science," she invited the woman to lunch pretending to be interested in the topic.

> Much to my dismay, she told me that the New Age Movement was far larger than that book portrayed it as being. That worried me, for Ms. Ferguson had described the Movement as being so large that it had kept me awake worrying several nights. I had heard enough! It was time to share my true feelings with her. I explained that my research combined with Bible studies had convinced me that this was the Movement of the Antichrist. To my surprise she agreed.... Complimenting me on my perceptiveness, she told me that I should also remember that in the New Age Movement as well as Unity, which is a part of the Movement, they believe Jesus and the Christ are two distinct entities.... She suggested I pray for wisdom to help me see the "hidden meaning" of those Bible passages .... Then to my surprise I heard her say: "It's just not right—not right. That book should not be allowed! It's too misleading!" Unable to believe my ears, I asked what book she was referring to and she exclaimed: "The Bible!"[7]

This would certainly be a disturbing lunch conversation! But it is only one example, albeit a vivid one. To Constance Cumbey it was proof of a large conspiracy paving the way for the Antichrist. But is this lunch guest the tip of a sinister iceberg or just someone who exists on the fringe of society seeking an identity and a place to belong? It is easy to overgeneralize from one anecdote.

41

Extremists on both fronts use vivid anecdotes to support their cases. Consider the following testimonial, found in a catalog entitled *Gateways to Self Discovery.*

> I purchased BUILD A WINNING SELF-IMAGE and I just realized that I don't have bad days anymore. When I'm having a "bad" day that is what most people would call a "good" day, and my good days are Fantastic Great Days! Thank you for showing me a better way.

It is important to realize that vivid examples are not proof in themselves. Vivid anecdotes are effective illustrations, but they can also ambush us and distort our thinking.

The Correlation Error

Misusing statistics is another way people come to faulty conclusions. One common problem is mistaking causation with correlation. To illustrate, consider the finding that nonsmokers get higher grades in college. This is a very appealing finding, at least to nonsmokers. But what can be concluded from this correlation? That smoking clouds not only your lungs but also your mind? Or could it be that, given the evidence on smoking, one has to have a clouded mind to smoke in the first place? Each of these is equally likely. It is also possible that a third variable may account for the relationship between the other two. It may be that someone who does not take scholarship seriously may pay as little attention to textbooks as to the warning label on cigarette packages.

When two things occur together, it is tempting to assume they are causally related. Two researchers in the early 1980s reported that rich people live longer than poor people. We might conclude that money makes one live longer, but many other explanations are possible. Maybe the wealthy can afford better medical treatment. Perhaps those with money are less exposed to infectious diseases because of lifestyle differences. Correlational findings are not easily interpreted.

This tendency to confuse correlation with causation is sometimes seen in extremist writings. Kilpatrick, an educational psychologist, succumbs to the correlation error in *Psychological Seduction*. He notes that the number of those with psychological problems has grown at the same time as the number of helpers. Kilpatrick writes:

> It sometimes seems there is a direct ratio between the increasing number of helpers and the increasing number of those who need help. The more psychologists we have, the more mental illness we get; the more social workers and probation officers, the more crime; the more teachers, the more ignorance.[8]

Though Kilpatrick recognizes the weakness in correlation, he concludes there must be some relationship between the two. But other factors correlate with the growth of social problems including the national debt, population growth, urbanization, and even Robert Schuller's ministry. Surely Kilpatrick would not blame the increase in social problems on Robert Schuller, and yet his ministry's growth would produce a similar correlation.

Mel and Norma Gabler make a similar correlational error in discussing the relationship between sex education and immorality.

> "...numerous studies and reports show that teenage promiscuity increases as the number of sex education courses taught in public schools increases. Teenage pregnancy also has jumped alarmingly—the very phenomenon educators promised sex ed would reduce!"[9]

It could be the Gablers are right that sex education classes encourage promiscuity. But it could also be that increasing promiscuity creates a need for sex education. Or it could be that increasing amounts of sex on television produce both increased promiscuity and increased awareness of sex and, as a result, pressure for sex education classes. Correlations are beautiful in their simplicity but can seduce us away from accurate conclusions.

Many look at the content of a persuasive message but fail to examine the logic. Sex education is an important issue in our schools. Critics charge it teaches physiology but not morality, while supporters point out that sex education is not taking place in the home as its critics want. Ironically, both advocates and critics use teenage pregnancy rates as support for their position. Correlations do not answer questions; they only suggest places to look for answers.

The Problem of Self-justification _____ 43

In the early 1950s Marion Keech began to receive messages from a race of friendly space people called the "Guardians" who warned her of the imminent destruction of the earth. She shared her messages with friends, and slowly a group of followers developed, calling themselves "The Seekers." As the day of the disaster approached, Ms. Keech received a message from the Guardians promising to rescue a few earthlings from the disaster. On the day of the pending disaster the Seekers gathered at Ms. Keech's house to await the flying saucer that would take them away. Midnight came, the time for delivery, and nothing happened.

One might expect the Seekers would become aware of their folly, admitting the Guardians did not exist. Instead, Ms. Keech announced the earth had been spared the disaster because of the faithfulness of the Seekers. A news conference was called, and interviews were granted to spread the good news. Instead of breaking up, the group was drawn more tightly together, their beliefs strengthened.[10]

The Seekers responded in the same way that each of us do to lesser inconsistencies. Whenever our actions and beliefs about ourselves contradict, we experience anxiety. It is then necessary to reduce the anxiety caused by the contradiction. Rather than admit that there were no messages and spaceships, the Seekers chose to justify their actions by adding a third belief—because of their actions the earth had been spared. Unfortunately, self-justification can blind us to reality.

The back cover of *The Hidden Dangers of the Rainbow* carries a replica of a full-page ad run worldwide on April 25, 1982. This ad proclaims that "The Christ is now here" and has been emerging since 1977 as a world educator. The author of the book, Constance Cumbey, identifies the world educator as the Antichrist and the New Age Movement as an organization that has infiltrated and paved the way for him. It is now seven years after the proclamation, yet we do not see the Antichrist. Cumbey admits to being perplexed by this and writes, "Although the full-page newspaper ads said Maitreya (the Antichrist) would soon appear, he has not done so yet. This worries me."[11] Since the Antichrist has not yet appeared, she reasons, it must mean he is the real Antichrist (not one of the many false Christs). His delay in appearing must be a result of God holding him back until the time is right. With this creative use of logic Cumbey justifies her beliefs, rather than changing them and avoiding the unpleasant possibility that she may have been wrong.

We all want to feel that our beliefs are based on solid evidence and sound reasoning. But social psychologists tell us that it often works the other way around. We believe something first and then find evidence to support our beliefs. Once persuaded to an extreme position, people often distort reality to fit existing beliefs. History is replete with such examples. Montanus predicted the Second Coming in the second century and gathered his followers at a spot near the modern capital of Turkey. The Anabaptists set 1533 as the date of the Second Coming. Sabbataie Zevi predicted 1648 and then 1666 as the years for the Second Coming before converting from Judaism to Islam. William Miller set 1843-1844 as his target range and gathered a large number of followers (the "Millerites") around him to await the event. Each of these would-be prophets proved to be wrong, yet their followers showed a renewed faith after the predictions failed.[12]

Those who produce and sell pornography sometimes justify their actions by arguing that pornography actually reduces sexual crimes. Customers take care of their sexual needs by looking at magazines or videos, they reason, instead of acting in sexually inappropriate ways. Alfred Hitchcock had a similar view of television violence. He believed those watching violence on television would be less likely to act out their violent fantasies than those not watching television. Hitchcock believed television put murder back in the living room where it belongs. The best current evidence suggests both the producers of pornography and Hitchcock are wrong. Viewing violence or sex does not seem to prevent acting out similar impulses. Those promoting pornography and television violence want to justify their businesses and end up distorting reality to do so.

Those who commit themselves to extreme positions may later find it difficult to believe any other way since it would mean changing basic beliefs. It is hard enough for us to admit little errors. Admitting extreme errors is even more difficult.

45

Self-fulfilling Prophecies

If teachers are led to believe that some students will perform better than others in the classroom, the selected students actually start doing better.[13] Teachers who believe that their students will perform better spend more time with them, teach them more, smile more at them, nod more when they are answering, and so on. If we expect excellence from someone, we may get it. If we expect hostility, we may get it.

Calvin Ellery was a paranoid schizophrenic who experienced delusions and hallucinations, believing the Masons were plotting to take over the government. He believed, moreover, that the Masons had discovered his knowledge of their intentions, and because he was a potential informer, the Masons had determined to do away with him. After misinterpreting certain things on a news broadcast, Ellery believed it was the day for his execution. When a salesman with a Masonic button on his lapel came to the front door, he was sure that the salesman had been sent to kill him. When the salesman reached into his pocket for his business card, Ellery assumed he was reaching for a revolver. Ellery drew his own weapon and shot first in self-defense.[14] This is a vivid example, so it must be interpreted with caution. It illustrates the power of the self-fulfilling prophecy. Ellery expected hostility from the salesman, and he perceived what he expected.

Self-fulfilling prophecy may also be used to explain Robert Schuller's and Norman Vincent Peale's results with positive mental attitude (PMA), which they advocate as a mental, emotional, and spiritual tool. With egos bolstered by the positive belief that something good will happen, positive thinkers may attempt ventures which they previously avoided. Since "nothing ventured is nothing gained," simply trying new things may produce increased success. The effectiveness of PMA need not be labelled satanic or interpreted in some mysterious fashion. For those expecting PMA to lead to success, it might actually work simply because it adds to their confidence.

But not all problems can be solved with greater confidence or a positive attitude. It is important to remember the vividness effect while considering the effectiveness of PMA. Perhaps only a small fraction of the people who use PMA become wealthy and famous, and it is this minority that gets the publicity and writes the books. Using their personal success and the success of a few followers as vivid examples, the advocates of PMA may be combining self-fulfilling prophecy with the vividness effect to persuade people to their beliefs.

Believing Is Seeing

One of the persistent phenomena in the study of thinking is the tendency for beliefs to determine what kind of information we seek out and how we interpret that information. For example, after purchasing a new car we tend to seek out ads that confirm our decision to purchase that particular car but avoid ads that highlight the good qualities of a competing car. Similarly, once we adopt a perspective, even if it is wrong, we will naturally seek out information that confirms our belief and avoid information that disconfirms it. One study showed that nonsmokers were twice as likely to read an article linking smoking with lung cancer than smokers.[15]

In *The Humanist*, William Thornton argues that religion does more harm than good and uses as an example the case of Fumiko Kumura, a Japanese immigrant who murdered her two sons by drowning them. Thornton writes about this case, "After learning that her husband was unfaithful, Kumura subordinated her maternal love and her obvious good nature to the authority of her religio-cultural tradition, which categorically demanded her suicide . . . Secular values would never have taken her into that surf . . . ."[16] Few religious people would have seen this bizzare tragedy as a good example of obedience to God, and yet Thornton uses it to represent religion.

When humanists like Thornton look at religion, they see tragedies like the Kumura case, book burnings, denominational infighting, TV preachers who accept credit card donations, and evangelists who claim that the *Mr. Ed* theme song has a backmasked satanic message. When Christians look at religion they see people feeding and clothing the poor, churches working for peace and justice, defenders of the unborn, and the moral backbone of the country. Seeing the best in yourself and the worst in others is normal. Unfortunately, it can leave us too nearsighted and defensive to see when the critics are right.

Constance Cumbey believes the New Age Movement is fulfilling all the prophecies concerning the Second Coming. Since she is convinced this movement is paving the way for the Antichrist, her beliefs influence how she interprets information. For example, Revelation 13:13-15 reads:

47

And he performed great and miraculous signs, even causing fire to come down from heaven to earth in full view of men. Because of the signs he was given power to do on behalf of the first beast, he deceived the inhabitants of the earth. He ordered them to set up an image in honor of the beast who was wounded by the sword and yet lived. He was given power to give breath to the image of the first beast, so that it could speak and cause all who refused to worship the image to be killed.

Cumbey reports being puzzled by the prophecy until she heard that the "Movement has devoted a great deal of research and attention to the use of holographic images."[17] She notes that one of the leaders of the New Age Movement commented that laser beam projectors have been placed on the top of one of their buildings. This is further proof to her that this is the movement of the Antichrist since these lasers are intended to bounce holographic images off satellites to fulfill the prophecy. Someone with a different set of beliefs would undoubtedly fail to make the connection she makes between the prophecy in Revelation and the supposed interest of the movement in lasers and holography.

We need to look beyond a single source or a single person for our beliefs and make sure that when we take our positions we are as fully informed as possible.

Avoiding Ambushes

What can be done to develop resistance to mental ambushes? The first step is to understand that it happens. Awareness is power — power to resist and to allow us to think critically. In addition to awareness, there are two specific ways we can improve our objectivity when reading or listening to what seem to be extreme positions.

Looking for other explanations. Looking for alternative explanations helps us sift through the claims of extremists. For example, in *What Are They Teaching Our Children?* the Gablers persuasively quote from textbooks to make their point that history texts are slandering America. One text has the following passage:

> "No nation on earth is guilty of practices more shocking and bloody than is [The United States of America]. . . . compare your facts with the everyday practices of this nation. Then you will agree with me that, for revolting barbarity and shameless hypocrisy, [The United States of America] has no rival."[18]

In evaluating the Gablers' reference list, one notices that the sources cover a wide time frame in the world of textbook publishing, mostly between 1970 and 1983, a thirteen-year range. This suggests two possibilities. One possibility is that these kinds of anti-American quotations are few and far between, and that the Gablers had to gather them over a long period of time to make their point. A second possibility is that they selected the quotes in this fashion to show the breadth of the problem.

A second discovery from the reference section is that the quote above is from a speech given by Frederick Douglass before the Civil War. Douglass is famous as a black abolitionist and was speaking against slavery. Understanding the quote in its context gives a different meaning from the one the Gablers projected. Even though the Gablers point out in the reference section that his speech is presented in the present tense, considering this anti-American seems questionable. Students need to be introduced to critical self-evaluation in order to learn from the mistakes of history. Depending on when and how the views of America are introduced, critical material can be appropriate.

Remember the vividness effect. The quote from Frederick Douglass is powerful anti-American rhetoric, but it was spoken in the age of slavery. It is vivid and undoubtedly persuasive, but is it an accurate representation of the bias of that particular textbook?

The quotes used by the Gablers will elicit different reactions from different people. Not all of the quotes will offend all readers, nor will they be seen as misrepresenting America. The Gablers are right to be concerned if students are being bombarded with anti-American propaganda from first grade on, but introducing older children to different perspectives of America is appropriate. A thoughtful critique of America and its policies can help inoculate students against extremist positions they will confront later.

It appears there is reason to be concerned about the portrayal of America in textbooks. But many of the textbooks the Gablers reviewed were written in the seventies — an era of self-criticism in America. Textbooks relate history, but they also reflect the age in which they were written and the educational philosophy of the writers. Textbooks written in the seventies undoubtedly reflected the doubt and insecurity of that era.

In their book critiquing American education, the Gablers clearly expressed their belief that history texts slander America and attack traditional American values and patriotism. They may be right, but it is important for readers to be aware of possible alternative explanations so that their conclusions can be critically evaluated.

Taking a historical perspective. Historical research can also help put the claims of extremists in perspective. The New Age conspiracy, for example, takes on a different light when looked at historically. The cover of *The Hidden Dangers of the Rainbow* proclaims it to be a "#1 Bestseller" and warns of the dangers of the imminent New Age. But a little history puts the New Age in a different perspective.

If the origins of the New Age Movement are traced to its roots, one finds Emanuel Swedenborg (1688-1772), who published the book *Arcana Coelestia* in 1749. This book was a collection of his conversations with angels. He, too, believed that the age of the Christian church was about to be overthrown, as foretold in Revelation, and that the new age would begin. Following in the tradition of Swedenborg, Andrew Jackson Davis, the "Seer of Poughkeepsie," wrote a book while in a trance (1845), demonstrated clairvoyant powers (reading newspapers blindfolded), and diagnosed diseases with his psychic powers. Jackson, like Swedenborg and Cumbey, believed that the new age was imminent—an age of social and religious revolution. In 1858, *The New York Times* reported on a convention of spiritualists in Chautauqua County, New York. Their goal, like those before and so many after, was to create a "Divine Social State upon Earth." None of these new ages came to be.

Then and now, those involved in movements like these tend to be social reformers dissatisfied with society and organized religion. As they band together they mutually reinforce beliefs in their powers. But as we have seen, predictions of new ages are notoriously inaccurate, and those sounding the alarm over the New Age Movement today need to take a historical perspective on such predictions. Even some modern experts on the New Age Movement are cautious about making Second Coming predictions. Douglas Groothuis, author of *Unmasking the New Age*, describes Cumbey's book as "an

50

implausible application of biblical prophecy to the New Age" and suggests it is "an unlikely conspiracy theory."[19] There is a New Age Movement, but perhaps a better name for today's version would be the "New New Age Movement."

Along with the New Age Movement, we are hearing about "mind power." Advocates claim the mind is capable of great things. While some talk of ESP, others praise products designed to take advantage of subliminal pathways to the mind. One catalog advertises mind-power cassettes to lose weight, stop smoking, boost willpower, make more money, remain faithful to one's spouse, and have super sex.

Mind power has a long history and has never been proven successful. *Scientific American* offered a $5,000 prize in 1922 for "conclusive psychic manifestations."[20] The investigation panel included, among others, Harry Houdini, William McDougal, a well-known psychologist, and J. Malcolm Bird, associate editor of *Scientific American*. After extensive testing of candidates, all panel members concluded no psychic power had been demonstrated. *Scientific American* repeated the challenge from 1941 to 1943 with a $10,000 prize and was equally unsuccessful in finding a legitimate case of psychic powers. British psychologist C. E. M. Hansel summed up the research on psychic powers this way: "After a hundred years of research, not a single individual has been found who can demonstrate ESP to the satisfaction of independent investigators. . . . The aim of parapsychology should be to produce one individual who can give a reliable and repeatable demonstration of ESP."[21] Contemporary research, as discussed in Chapter 1, indicates subliminal message tapes are no more effective than ESP.

The research on human thinking is fascinating, although at times discouraging. It seems that we seldom, if ever, can think clearly, free from all bias and distortion. David Myers, a Christian psychologist and author, sums it up this way:

> Knowing our susceptibility to erroneous belief also has implications for our view of ourselves. First, it cautions us, 'Judge not.' Since our judgments of others are readily susceptible to error, we can easily wrong people when we spread our judgments . . . . Second, we ought not take ourselves too seriously, nor should we feel intimidated by

51

people who are unwavering 'true believers.' The temptation to think more of ourselves and our wisdom than we ought is ever present. If illusory thinking taints all domains of human belief, then it is bound to contaminate my ideas and yours, and the next person's too.[22]

Knowing something about our own tendency to err can tell us something important about those who presume to know truth. Much truth is knowable, but approaching it is fraught with dangers of intellectual ambush.

Quiz Answers

1. Deaths from strokes occur almost twice as much as deaths from accidents.
2. More than twice as many people die from heart disease than from cancer.
3. Neither are likely. There were four deaths from smallpox vaccinations and one from botulism during the year this information was compiled.
4. Death from asthma is almost twice as common as death from electrocution.
5. More than twice as many die from diabetes as die from homicides, although the number of homicides in Washington, D.C., exceeded the number of deaths resulting from the uprising in the West Bank and Gaza Strip during a recent fifteen-month period.
6. Digestive system cancer claimed more lives than motor vehicle accidents.
7. There were 44 deaths from tornados and 163 from excess cold during the year these data were compiled.
8. Death from appendicitis was eight times more likely than death by lightning.
9. More than twice as many died from tuberculosis as from vehicle/train collisions.
10. Leukemia claimed almost twice as many lives as drowning.

CHAPTER FOUR

The Dangers of Believing Without Thinking

Tuesday, January 28, 1986. A cold front had moved into southern Florida dropping temperatures below freezing. Morton Thiokol engineers were worried about the effect of the low temperatures on the shuttle Challenger's booster-rocket seals. Launch temperature was forecast to be 29 degrees and the lowest previous launch temperature had been 53 degrees. The engineers were being pressured by management to make a launch recommendation, even while they disagreed over the danger of launching. Finally a launch decision was made. At 11:38 a.m. the Challenger lifted off. Shortly after lift-off the seals in the right booster failed and the rocket exploded, killing all seven astronauts aboard. In the launch viewing stands were the children and relatives of the astronauts, and thousands more children were watching on TV, since one of the astronauts was Christa McAuliffe, who was to be the first teacher in space.

Freezethink: The Danger of Believing Too Soon ――――――

In an analysis of the shuttle disaster, psychologist Arie Kruglanski identified a phenomenon known as "freezethink" in which the decision-making process is cut off before completion. In normal decision making the person or group gathers information, considers and weighs different opinions, and then selects an action. But in the case of the Challenger accident, Kruglanski believes the decision-making process was cut off prematurely.

Kruglanski's analysis focused on the motivational factors involved in making the launch decision.[1] The presence of contradictory information was insufficient to overcome the powerful need to have a launch decision. Imagine a comparable situation among Christians:

Bob and Rhonda have been Christians since childhood. They are trying to raise their children in the same way. But sometimes secular forces seem overwhelming. Their school-age children face more obstacles than Bob and Rhonda did as children. Humanism has influenced education, rock music lyrics are more explicitly immoral than in the past, and prime-time television advocates promiscuity and violence. Bob and Rhonda look for help. They feel unprepared in a challenging world.

Their need to have a strong position in the face of such adversity is understandable. Unfortunately, sometimes the need for a strong position overpowers the need to have a well-reasoned position. Once accepted, the extreme position becomes entrenched and Bob and Rhonda will be inclined to believe without thinking — the act of freezethinking. Kruglanski identifies three particular motivational forces involved in freezethink.

Need for a Positive Conclusion. We usually want a positive conclusion to life experiences. We want a happy ending for every sixty-minute television program. We expect the books we read to leave us smiling. We want our children to succeed in life. We all want to be above average in our work and parenting responsibilities. Yet, distressingly enough, positive conclusions are more common on television than in real life.

Before the Challenger launch, there had been pressure on NASA to make the shuttle pay for itself and to keep up a regular launch schedule. Every system failure and delay gave the program bad publicity. Jobs depended on the success of the shuttle. Every worker in the program wanted the shuttle to launch on schedule, thereby avoiding another disappointment. The launch decision fit with the hopes of NASA. The employees of the Morton Thiokol Corporation were similarly engaged in wishful thinking since Thiokol received $400 million of business per year from NASA. The launch decision fit with their wishes.

Bob and Rhonda want a happy ending for their children. So, after reading books on the dangers of modern society, they might sell their television, home-school their children, and discard their children's records and tapes. Their actions might follow the recommendations of the authors they read, but it would also be important to think through the potential consequences of these actions. How likely is it that selling the television will successfully prevent children from exposure to immoral values?

Christians searching for help with the difficult issues of today want to believe there are answers to their questions. Extremists often claim there are easy answers that they have discovered. "Read these passages from Scripture, understand them the way I do, believe the way I do, and you will see clearly." Accepting extreme answers allows the beleaguered Christian to resolve an issue and expect a happy ending.

Cognitive Structure. A second powerful motivating force is the desire to have cognitive structure, a clear set of thoughts on an issue. We are uncomfortable with ambiguity. Unresolved conflicts cause stress, and stress motivates us to find solutions. Under enough stress, any position will look better than no position.

In the case of the decision to launch the Challenger, those making the decision were faced with an ambiguous situation. There were concerns about launching in cold weather, but no one knew for sure it would be a problem. As the launch deadline grew nearer the need for cognitive structure grew stronger, eventually reaching the point where any decision was better than no decision.

The psychological equivalent of a *launch deadline* is the pressure we feel to make a decision or take a stand on an issue. Bob and Rhonda, for example, may feel that if they don't make drastic changes in their lifestyle, their children are destined for ruin.

Adding to the ambiguity problem is the fact that we often don't have well-thought-out positions on issues. Psychologist Daryl Bem believes that people spend most of their lives in such a state, a state where their minds are made up of opinion molecules. The molecules are discrete bits and pieces of positions on issues. Each molecule is made up of a fact, a feeling, and a following. If asked for an opinion on a national value-added tax, one may feel a need to respond although he or she

55

may have no well-reasoned position. People want to appear knowledgeable and to be involved in conversations. In order to respond we access our opinion molecules. In one molecule there is a memory of hearing Uncle Joe say that "value-added taxes are just another sales tax and a hidden one at that!" Accompanying that *fact* is a *feeling* of respect for Uncle Joe. And a lot of family members respected Uncle Joe. He had a good *following*. Based on this, one might respond in opposition to a value-added tax, "It is just a hidden sales tax."

On some issues, such as the value-added tax, we may have no position until we are pressed to respond. And the more pressed we are, the greater the need to resolve the issue. Pressing someone on an issue is like creating a launch deadline, making us more and more uncomfortable with psychological ambiguities. When we reach a point where any decision is better than no decision, we are especially vulnerable to the claims of extremists.

Imagine Bob and Rhonda as they watch a Christian evangelist on television charge, "Public schools corrupt our children because public schools are run by secular humanists." As the evangelist speaks the camera pans the audience, showing looks of approval. In that brief moment Bob and Rhonda have been exposed to fact, feeling, and following. Because they are looking for cognitive structure, they may find the argument convincing even though no convincing arguments have been presented. The conspiracy and catastrophe theories of Christian extremists are appealing to those seeking cognitive structure.

Inadequate Fear of Invalidity. Fearing a bad decision can be a good critical thinking skill. Although fear can grow and hinder or even defeat the decision maker, a little fear can introduce appropriate caution. That fear of making a wrong decision (invalidity) was overcome in the Challenger decision by a general enthusiasm for the launch. No one wanted to think about the consequences of a wrong decision.

One couple may contemplate whether to take on extra work in order to send their children to a private school rather than having them continue at the public school. It is a difficult decision, with advantages and disadvantages on both sides. They fear making the wrong decision. Because of their uncertainties, they visit public and private schools, comparing the education and teaching styles. They discuss the problem with their pastor, friends, and family. Eventually they decide to take on part-time employment and send their children to a private school.

Another couple reads a book that states the public schools are run by anti-Christian secular humanists who want to remove all Christian values from society. They immediately make decisions regarding their employment and family budget that will make money available in order to enroll their children in a private school.

Both couples made the same decision. The first used good critical thinking skills, but the second had an inadequate fear of invalidity and made a rushed decision.

When decisions are not approached with a healthy fear of invalidity, the decision maker is vulnerable to prepackaged conclusions of others. Rather than making a personal decision, it is sometimes easier to blindly follow the advice of a prominent Christian. Freezethink stifles critical thinking.

Groupthink: The Danger of Substituting Agreement for Belief

One of the strategies for preventing freezethink, discussed later in this chapter, is to make group decisions rather than individual decisions. For example, churches that make group decisions usually have better leadership than churches led by a single individual. But groups also face dangers in forming opinions and making decisions.

In the 1960s President Kennedy and his advisors thought that one small brigade could overthrow Castro's communist regime and supported an invasion of Cuba. The troops landed at the Bay of Pigs and were soon surrounded and trapped. The world reacted negatively to the invasion. Later Kennedy wondered how he and his advisors could have been so foolish.

Psychologist Irving Janis believes Kennedy and his advisors were victims of *groupthink*, the kind of thinking people use when group consensus becomes more important than a realistic appraisal of the situation. In the Bay of Pigs decision, maintaining consensus caused the group to overlook and underestimate certain information. Groupthink is likely

57

whenever a leader gathers a group of like-minded supporters to help make decisions. Each member of the group supports and validates the others. A mutual admiration society is formed, and the group loses touch with reality. Groupthink can happen in government, in industry, in groups as diverse as the ACLU and the Aryan Nations, and in Christian organizations.

Christian groupthink is likely when Christian leaders gather a group of similarly believing Christians who begin to mutually reinforce one another's beliefs. As the group members reinforce each other they become more and more convinced that they are right and others are wrong. "After all," they reason, "look at all the other fine Christians in my group that believe the same way." The group, convinced that it knows the truth, becomes intolerant of the views of others. With more isolation there is less chance of being exposed to information that would upset the groupthink.

Janis believes there are symptoms of groupthink that can only be identified by those on the outside:

1. *A sense of invulnerability.* Groupthink leads to the belief that the group can do no wrong and that no harm can come to it. For example, John F. Kennedy and his advisors underestimated the world reaction to the U.S.-sponsored invasion of Cuba because they neglected to assess potential harm when making their decision. Similarly, the admiral in command of Pearl Harbor and his fellow officers failed to prepare for attack because of a sense of invulnerability. After losing contact with the Japanese aircraft carriers that were headed toward Hawaii, he joked that the carriers could be rounding Diamond Head and we wouldn't know it.

Scandals in the 1980s among television evangelists illustrate the sense of invulnerability. Each of these leaders engaged in behavior that was inappropriate, and yet each apparently felt immune from public scrutiny. When the first scandal broke, the second minister pointed the finger and condemned the first. Eventually, he fell, too.

Denominational divisions cause some to feel invulnerable. When a member of one denomination insults another denomination because of doctrinal differences — infant baptism, pre-tribulation rapture, gifts of the Spirit, or style of leadership — it demonstrates a sense of invulnerability that comes from being part of an organized group. The same individual would be much less haughty if he or she were not surrounded by others with a similar set of beliefs.

2. *Rationalization.* Groups exhibiting groupthink have a tendency to ignore warnings, partly because they feel invulnerable and partly because they have constructed rationalizations to account for their inconsistencies. These rationalizations allow them to stay committed to the original decision. The commander of the naval base at Pearl Harbor convinced himself that the Japanese would never attack the harbor and risk a war with the United States because they would surely lose such a war. Kennedy and his advisors convinced themselves that the Cuban people could not support a communist government and, when given the opportunity, would overthrow the government of Castro.

The rationalizations among Christian extremists tend to be circular: You don't agree with me because you don't understand the message of Scripture. How will you know when you have properly understood Scripture? When you agree with me.

The positive-thinking doctrine of Norman Vincent Peale provides another example of rationalization. "Everything is possible for him who believes" (Mark 9:23b) is a verse Peale quotes in suggesting we will get the best if we expect it. In addition to being circular (one measures positive thinking by happiness and happiness is available through positive thinking), this position ignores many other passages about the value of pain and growth through trials. Paul unsuccessfully requested deliverance from a "thorn in the flesh" and eventually concluded that God's power was magnified through Paul's weakness (2 Corinthians 12:7-9).

3. *Morality.* A manslaughter trial in Portland, Oregon, in 1989 demonstrated the tragic effects of groupthink. Staff members of the Ecclesia Athletic Association, a group living arrangement for inner-city youth, were convicted of beating the group leader's daughter to death. The victim allegedly bit a staff member and eluded discipline. Her punishment beatings were spread over two evenings while the other children were required to watch. After the punishment, she was draped across an open window sill where she suffocated. The beatings

59

that were routinely used to punish the children were justified by the leader of the group; they would teach behavior that would cause them to avoid much worse punishment in adulthood. Under the guise of discipline and morality, staff members killed a child.

Groupthinkers believe they have found the moral highground. Believing they are morally superior makes it possible for them to minimize or ignore the ethical consequences of their actions.

The moral superiority of groupthink victims gives them the confidence to dismiss issues that others would not take so lightly. Janis uses the decisions about bombing North Vietnam to illustrate this.

> .. during 1966 President Johnson's ingroup was concerned primarily with selecting bomb targets in North Vietnam. They based their selections on four factors—the military advantage, the risk to American aircraft and pilots, the danger of forcing other countries into the fighting, and the danger of heavy civilian casualties. At their regular Tuesday luncheons, they weighed these factors the way schoolteachers grade examination papers, averaging them out. Though evidence on this point is scant, I suspect that the group's ritualistic adherence to a standardized procedure induced the members to feel morally justified in their destructive way of dealing with the Vietnamese people—after all, the danger of heavy civilian casualties from U.S. air strikes was taken into account on their checklists.[2]

Some politicians argue that the cause of democracy justifies supporting conflict in other countries. Opponents believe life is more valuable than democracy. Each group believes it has a higher morality than the other.

The same process occurs in Christian thinking. Conservatives try to uphold moral order. They get involved in politics and lobby for morality in television programming and court decisions. Liberals get involved in ecumenical efforts, world hunger relief, and civil rights movements. Each group believes it is more moral than the other. The crossfire continues.

4. *Stereotypes.* Another symptom of groupthink is the tendency to stereotype the leaders of other groups and engage in sloganistic thinking. Opposition leaders are viewed as evil

or stupid. President Johnson's decisions about bombing North Vietnam occurred in an atmosphere of sloganistic thinking where phrases like "the communist apparatus" and "domino theory" permeated the group. At Pearl Harbor the navy commanders naively thought of Japan as "a midget that would not dare strike a blow against a powerful giant."[3]

In Christian circles we hear about "secular humanists," "New Agers," "agents of the Antichrist," "falling away," and other slogans. Leaders of liberal Christian groups or non-Christian groups are seen as evil and misleading. Conversely, leaders of conservative Christian groups are stereotyped as closed-minded, intolerant, and stupid.

5. *Pressure and self-censorship.* The groupthink atmosphere is maintained partly because any member that disagrees with the group is immediately put under pressure. The group's goal is consensus rather than good decision making. Dissenters are pressured not to express doubts to outsiders. This keeps the illusion of unanimity and allows the group to bring the dissenter into line.

The dissenter is also pressured to keep the dissent within acceptable bounds of deviation. The limits of dissent are clear to the entire group, and the members individually censor what they say in order to fit within group boundaries. Dissent appears more like weak support than true dissent. Furthermore, silence is erroneously interpreted as agreement. There is comfort in agreement, but groupthink often leads to poor decisions.

Avoiding Christian Freezethink and Groupthink

Several recommendations for preventing freezethink and groupthink can also apply to Christians wanting to think critically in today's crossfire. These recommendations are designed to prevent the person or group from cutting off a decision-making process too soon.

Gather adequate information. The first step is to gather all the available information. In Chapter 3 we discussed the importance of looking for alternative explanations. This often requires checking references and sources.

61

"No nation on earth is guilty of practices more shocking and bloody than is [The United States of America]. . . . compare your facts with the everyday practices of this nation. Then you will agree with me that, for revolting barbarity and shameless hypocrisy, [The United States of America] has no rival." We used this example in Chapter 3 to show how out-of-context quotations can be misleading. Understanding that this was a statement made by an abolitionist during the Civil War gives it an entirely new perspective.

Hunt and McMahon's belief that psychologists have suppressed embarrassing research and that "There are many other skeletons in the psychotherapy closet—a closet that is kept tightly shut lest an unsuspecting public learn the truth" seems less credible when one discovers the research to which they refer has been widely distributed by the organization that was supposedly working to suppress it. Hunt and McMahon also cite Sigmund Koch, a well-known critic of psychology, who conducted a study and concluded psychology is not a science. After citing others who support this view, Hunt and McMahon write, "Any facts that would endanger the future of this huge industry [psychology] are kept as professional secrets among its members." But Hunt and McMahon found this secret information about psychology's fallibility in *Psychology Today*, professional journals available in libraries, and books available in most bookstores. It hardly seems like a cover-up scandal.

David Noebel, author of *The Marxist Minstrels: A Handbook on Communist Subversion of Music*, expresses concerns about a number of musicians including The Beattles, Woody Guthrie, and Bob Dylan. Noebel cites their associations with known communists and the fact that communists like much of the messages contained in folk music. In addition, communists have promoted the careers of some folk singers. Noebel writes, ". . . with time and assistance from leftist John Hammond, Columbia released his topical (pro-communist) songs . . . ." How was John Hammond identified as a leftist? Checking the reference, one finds his communist leanings were established by the House Committee on Un-American Activities, a committee now discredited and infamous for its communist witch-hunts. In the chapter on Bob Dylan, Noebel writes, "Irvin Silber, editor of *Sing Out!* and identified under oath as having been a member of the Communist Party, has both praised and condemned Dylan." Once again the House Committee on Un-American Activities is the source.

Gathering adequate information is an important step in avoiding freezethink and groupthink. If more information had been known about the cold-weather performance of the booster-rocket seals on the Challenger, a national tragedy could have been avoided. If more information about the Cuban people had been gathered before the Bay of Pigs invasion, an international incident could have been avoided. Similarly, if we explore varying perspectives on important issues, we will make better decisions.

Recognize the dangers of wrong decisions. A second way to prevent premature decision making is to develop a healthy fear of invalidity, frequently reminding ourselves of the consequences of our decisions. Taking toys away from our children, instructing others not to see psychologists, selling the television set, or changing churches because the pastor used guided meditation are all decisions that can have profound consequences, positive or negative. Fearing the consequences promotes better decision making.

A California lawsuit illustrates the need for fearing wrong decisions. A young man seeking pastoral counseling at a church committed suicide, and the family sued the church for not referring the man for professional help. There are many issues involved in this case, including the separation of church and state, the competency of seminary-trained counselors in treating serious mental illness, and the responsibility of counselors to predict suicidal behavior. But those arguing against professional psychology would do well to fear similar outcomes.

Seek diverse opinions. In regard to the shuttle disaster, Kruglanski recommended that "A judicious blending of those with different motivations — astronauts, engineers and managers — could create a climate for rational judgment." Those with a high need for structure are prone to accept any decision; those with an extremely high fear of invalidity may be unable to make a decision. Together, those with two conflicting motives can cancel each other out and produce a better decision than either individual. Groups comprised of those with different motives may have more conflict and disagreement, but the conflict is often a healthy hedge against groupthink.

In making decisions about controversial issues, it is wise to seek out those with different motives. The couple trying to decide whether to send their children to public or private school would do well to discuss the options with public and private school teachers. A variety of perspectives helps the critical thinker.

Another example of the need to seek out diverse points of view when making decisions is seen in the controversy over the content and impact of television. There are secular and Christian critics telling us television is the single most harmful force in society. One author called TV a "plug-in drug." Phil Phillips, author of *Turmoil in the Toybox*, believes children's programs are loaded with occult symbols. And concern has grown with the advent of cable TV. Christians from different denominations have become so disturbed by what they see on TV that they have formed a group called "Christian Leadership for Responsible Television" (CLRTV). The coalition is made up of 1,600 Christian leaders. These are important concerns, and Christians are right to be disturbed by immorality on television. But what other perspectives are there on television?

> . . . it isn't very fair to judge television only by its bad programs. We don't judge literature by the hundreds of mediocre plays and pedestrian poetry written by hacks of the day. Instead we look at the Chaucers, Shakespeares, or Miltons to gauge the literary achievement of a generation. We should judge today's television the same way, not by its worst but its best.[4]

64

Or how about this view of television?

> In 1977, over 130 million viewers tuned in to watch at least one of the segments of "Roots," the ABC television network's production of Alex Haley's history of several generations of a black family in America. The shows received widespread acclaim for promoting the awareness of black history and for inspiring blacks' pride in their heritage.[5]

Television has potential for harm and for good. Getting rid of the television set because of distasteful programming may be right for some families, but they would also lose the positive influence along with the negative. Seeking out different perspectives on an issue helps us come to a better understanding and make better decisions.

It is surprising but nevertheless true that groups with diverse points of view are often better than individuals at decision making. This is not good news to most people because we like others to be in agreement with us. In a group where multiple points of view are held, if a give-and-take process is not permitted to ensue, the members become frustrated or even stifled. Although a committee can wallow in disagreement and dispute trivial matters and its decisions may seem only slightly better than a compromise, it generally will make a better decision in spite of the difficulties. Groups have more perspectives than individuals, and the diversity of carefully constructed groups helps prevent groupthink. Despite the frustrations, group decision making is often superior to individual decision making. Consider the following example:

> It is approximately 10:00 a.m. in mid August and you have just crash landed in the Sonora Desert in southwestern United States. The light twin engine plane, containing the bodies of the pilot and the co-pilot, has completely burned.... The pilot was unable to notify anyone of your position before the crash.... The immediate area is quite flat and except for occasional barrel and saguaro cacti appears to be rather barren. The last weather report indicated the temperature would reach 110° that day, which means that the temperature at ground level will be 130°.[6]

This is the opening to a group exercise in which the decision-making abilities of individuals are compared to the abilities of a group. Individuals rank a number of items as to their importance for survival (e.g., salt tablets, knife, parachute, pint of water, etc.). The rank order that is assigned to the items reflects the knowledge, experience, and intuition of each individual. Next, the survivors meet in a group and agree on a group ranking of the items. This normally requires much discussion because the individual lists differ significantly. Finally, the group and individual lists are compared to that of an expert on desert survival. Almost always the group performance is superior to that of the individuals.

Groups make better decisions because the individuals pool their bits and pieces of information (opinion molecules). With more complete information a better decision can be made. Also, since we all see the world through our previous experiences, our various perspectives help cancel out untenable conclusions. King Solomon's wisdom is seen in his words, "Plans fail for lack of counsel, but with many advisors they succeed." (Proverbs 15:22)

In Deuteronomy 17:6 and 19:15, the importance of not depending on the perceptions of a single individual is emphasized: "One witness is not enough to convict a man accused of any crime or offense he may have committed. A matter must be established by the testimony of two or three witnesses." Jesus emphasized the importance of multiple perceptions in Matthew 18 when He taught:

> "If your brother sins against you, go and show him his fault, just between the two of you. If he listens to you, you have won your brother over. But if he will not listen, take one or two others along, so that every matter may be established by the testimony of two or three witnesses." (vv. 15, 16)

Because human perceptions can be distorted, multiple witnesses lend credibility.

The remedy for Christian freezethink and groupthink is awareness and appreciation of differing perspectives. Gathering more information, recognizing the dangers of wrong decisions, and seeking diverse opinions can help us think critically. We need the crossfire in order to find diversity, and we need critical thinking to avoid being captured by the groupthink at the extremes. Being aware of how our thought processes can prematurely freeze and the ways we can be ambushed (Chapter 3) makes us less susceptible and better able to avoid capture.

66

CHAPTER FIVE

The Shield
Of Critical Thinking

A husband and wife were preparing dinner. The wife took the roast out of the refrigerator, cut off a small part, and put the small piece back in the refrigerator. The husband said, "Honey, you do that whenever we have roast. Why?" She replied, "I don't know why, it's the way my mother always did it." Curious, the wife called her mother and asked why she always cut off part of the roast when she prepared it for dinner. Her reply was, "I don't know why, but that's the way my mother always did it." Even more curious now, the wife called her grandmother and asked the same question. The grandmother was silent for a moment, and then said, "I don't know about you or your mother, but my pan was too small."

This story illustrates the trap of believing without thinking. As Christians we can fall into the same trap and follow our leaders blindly. On the battlefield of ideas this is an understandable reaction to the confusion of the two-front war. Regrettably, hiding in our ideological bunkers can cause the problems described in the previous chapters.

But just as believing without thinking is a problem, it is also a problem to think without believing. If it is possible to live without believing in anyone or anything, it is most certainly a tragic existence without structure or meaning. And we cannot simply dismiss all extremists and their unusual positions, because God sometimes uses extremists to discover truth.

> . . . no matter how much fundamentalist groups may misrepresent what we understand to be the Christian faith, they can all reveal something genuine about the faith — something that, without their witness, is obscured. There is an old adage to the effect that extreme Christian groups

or sects are the church's unpaid bills. They represent issues with which the church hasn't fully come to terms.[1]

Extreme ideas tend to be built around partial truths. The difficulty is finding the truth without being swept away by prevailing groupthink. Extremists help us identify truth, but we need to shield ourselves with critical thinking in the process.

A Critical Need for Critical Thinking

An interview on a radio station illustrates the importance of critical thinking. The person being interviewed claimed to be able to predict earthquakes, volcanic activity, and avalanches. The earthquakes were predicted by various aches and pains she felt in her body and avalanches by a tingling of the skin. Earaches meant one thing, headaches another, chest pains still another. Combinations of these and variations in intensity were all important to her predictions. These aches and pains would come on her and persist for days. Sure enough, after several days of aches and pains an earthquake would follow. After the earthquake the pains would subside until the next quake. She claimed by using her pains she had been able to predict a long list of earthquakes and volcanic eruptions. When asked if she had ever had pains that had failed to predict an earthquake she replied no, she always accurately predicted earthquakes. Sometimes, however, they did not occur in the location she predicted.

68 A critical thinker might question these claims. Developing aches and pains that persist until an earthquake occurs somewhere in the world is not the same thing as predicting earthquakes since earthquakes occur frequently. Also, earthquakes tend to occur more frequently in some areas than others because of geological structure, and pointing to those areas and predicting an earthquake is not particularly amazing. Predicting an earthquake in California next year or that volcanic activity will occur around Mt. St. Helens is quite safe.

It is surprising how vulnerable we are to suspending our critical thinking abilities, especially when faced with extraordinary or bizarre explanations. Kenneth Feder, a university professor, had this to say about his students:

Much of the time it seems as though our students cannot write, they cannot speak, and they do not read. A good proportion appear to sleep-walk through their classes, and the most cogent question you can elicit from them concerns whether or not the final exam is cumulative.

Like most colleges and universities, Feder's school regularly sponsors lectures and presentations on important social issues. Speakers had been invited to his campus to discuss the threat of nuclear war, the problem of hunger, and environmental concerns. Unless the faculty gave course credit for attending, the lectures were sparsely attended. However, when Feder's university hosted speakers on the existence of ghosts, a thousand students attended. Feder writes:

> For close to two hours, students who ordinarily display the intellectual curiosity of household appliances when we attempt to teach them literature, history, and science sat in rapt attention while the lecturers showed dozens of slides of alleged ghosts. To anyone with even a scintilla of rationality, not to mention just a measure of healthy skepticism, the pictures appeared to be double exposures and rather amateurish cut/and/paste jobs. Yet the crowd seemed willing to accept as genuine nearly every one of them.[2]

Feder's concern is not that the "used-car salesmen of the occult" were allowed to sell their ideas and their books. His concern is that the college students failed to think critically during the presentation. Feder notes that there are natural questions that should have arisen during the presentation. When the speakers claimed bioluminescence was a supernatural process enabling spirits to be visible, why didn't the students remember their biology course where they learned bioluminescence is a natural process by which fireflies produce light? Why wouldn't the students use their skills of deductive reasoning to discount the claims of the presenters when they noticed that these supposedly nonphysical ghosts cast shadows in the photographs? The ghosts were transparent images, but what about the clothing the ghosts were wearing? Was the clothing transparent because it was the spirit of dead clothes? When informed that ghosts appear at 3:00 a.m. as an "insult to the trinity," wouldn't students wonder which time zone ghosts use?

69

Feder's experience is not unique, nor is the lack of critical thinking unique to college students. The widespread belief in astrology is another example of a belief system that evaporates when critical thinking is applied. Studies of personality show no relationship between the astrological sign one is born under and personality, nor can astrologers reliably match personalities of people they meet with their signs. Despite the evidence that exists and the fact astrology defies common sense, it persists in being popular.

Part of the appeal of astrology and other persuasive rhetoric is because of the Barnum effect, named after P. T. Barnum, who is well-known for his dictum, "There's a sucker born every minute." To understand the Barnum effect, imagine being given a computer printout describing your personality based on your zodiac sign:

> You have a strong need for other people to like you and for them to admire you. You have a tendency to be critical of yourself. You pride yourself on being an independent thinker and do not accept other opinions without satisfactory proof. You have found it unwise to be too frank in revealing yourself to others. At times you are extroverted, affable, sociable, while at other times you are introverted, wary, and reserved. Some of your aspirations tend to be pretty unrealistic.[3]

This statement, drawn from an astrology book, is generally true for most people regardless of their zodiac sign. Because it is generally true, we tend to accept it as a valid description of our individual personalities—the Barnum effect. When given this bogus personality description, most rate it as a good summary of their personality. In fact, most report it to be more true than an individualized personality description based on an established personality test. Astrologers and other pseudoscientists count on the Barnum effect to make their statements believable.

Stuck Windows. We live in the age of relativism where we are taught our beliefs aren't better than those of our neighbors, just different. We are told the beliefs of conservatives aren't better than those of liberals, just different. We hear that the principles guiding our culture and nation are not better than those of other cultures and nations, just different. Instead of traditional virtues, today's values reflect a single virtue — openness. We are not taught to evaluate and judge, but simply to accept. Acceptance, not critical thinking, is considered the mark of a developed mind.

A mind trained to be open, accepting, and always withholding judgment is like a window stuck open. An open window lets in cool air but it also lets in wind, rain, sleet, and snow. The proper function of a window is to open and close depending on the weather. An open mind can be like an eternally open window. Instead of judging the merits of ideas and beliefs, the mind that has been stuck open lets everything in. Tales of ghosts or astrology have the same merit to the completely open person as theories of quantum mechanics or scriptural principles.

Allan Bloom in *The Closing of the American Mind* describes the substitution of openness for critical thinking.

> Openness — and the relativism that makes it the only plausible stance in the face of various claims to truth and various ways of life and kinds of human beings — is the great insight of our times. The true believer is the real danger. The study of history and of culture teaches that all the world was mad in the past; men always thought they were right, and that led to wars, persecutions, slavery, xenophobia, racism, and chauvinism. The point is not to correct the mistakes and really bé right; rather it is not to think you are right at all.[4]

Bloom regrets the fact that relativism has eliminated traditional American heroes and convinced many Americans that the principles on which we founded our country were racist. Our children have been left without heroes and without principles. Without belief in something, they have no yardstick by which to measure other ideas.

Bloom also argues that American culture has failed to provide fundamental education in religion. As such, we have missed an important basis for evaluation. He writes:

> The other element of fundamental primary learning that has disappeared is religion. As the respect for the Sacred — the latest fad — has soared, real religion and knowledge of the Bible have diminished to the vanishing point. The gods never walked very tall in our political life

71

or in our schools. The Lord's Prayer we mumbled in grade school when I was a child affected us less than the Pledge of Allegiance we also recited. It was the home—and the houses of worship related to it—where religion lived. The holy days and the common language and set of references that permeated most households constituted a large part of the family bond and gave it substantial .content. Moses and the Tablet of the Law, Jesus and his preaching of brotherly love, had an imaginative existence. Passages from the Psalms and the Gospels echoed in children's heads. Attending church or synagogue, praying at the table, were a way of life, inseparable from the moral education that was supposed to be the family's special responsibility in this democracy.[5]

Bloom despairs over the loss of fundamental religious education. Religious training provided people with a time-tested set of values and beliefs. This firm foundation allowed them to have a truly open mind—not a mind where any idea or belief is accepted without examination—an open critical mind where ideas are judged on their individual merits and not automatically accepted as having equal value with all other ideas.

Religious training is important, but it is not the complete solution to the crossfire problem. Just as total openness is like a window stuck open, a mind can also be stuck closed. Whether through freezethink, groupthink, or self-justification, many extremists have committed themselves to closed-mindedness. A window stuck closed impedes critical thinking just as a window stuck open does. Christian critical thinkers need to have windows that open *and* close, depending on the conditions outside.

The Evil Mind. Critical thinking is not prized by all Christians. Some believe our reasoning abilities are responsible for most of our problems. You have probably heard statements like the following, which are untrue, partially true, or that mislead: "Beginning with the Garden of Eden, humankind's problems have resulted when people reasoned for themselves instead of relying on God for guidance." "If Adam and Eve had followed God's instructions, and not thought for themselves, they would never have tasted the forbidden fruit." "Reasoning abilities have only served to contaminate the church and lead believers astray."

The charge that careful reasoning is unreliable and that only the Bible contains all truth has been made with adverse effects and serious consequences felt by many godly Christians. It is this mentality that has caused persecution of people, even persecution of Christians by Christians in acts like the Crusades, the Salem witch trials, the justification of slavery, the treatment of epileptics as though they had demons, and so on.

Martin and Deidre Bobgan have expressed concern about human wisdom in their book *Psychoheresy*. Psychology is dangerous, they suggest, because of "the use of the unproven and unscientific psychological opinions of men instead of absolute confidence in the biblical truth of God."[6] They quote a Christian in the eighteenth century:

> What is the source of all this spiritual blindness which from age to age thus mistakes and defeats all the gracious designs of God towards fallen mankind? Look at the origin of the first sin, and you have it all. Had Eve desired no knowledge but that which came from God, Paradise had still been the habitation of her and of all her offspring. . . .
> But now corruption, sin, death, and every evil of the world have entered into the Church . . . . And in the very same way, and from the same cause: namely, a desire for knowledge other than that which comes from the inspiration of the Spirit of God alone. This desire is the serpent's voice in every man . . . .[7]

Christians have a long history of discomfort with human reason. The concern that thinking abilities would lead humans astray became acute as the Renaissance began to remove knowledge from the control of those in authority. Instead of relying on the church for knowledge, people began to respect their own abilities and to think and see truth for themselves. Science was born and began the march toward technology, control of disease and environment, and exploration. The new respect for reason led to a loss of respect for those who had been in authority, including church authorities. Is it any wonder that human reason was suspect?

There have always been those who reject reason as a valid way of knowing. Tertullian (160-230), an early church theologian and apologist, rejected philosophy, which relied upon

73

reason. St. Bernard (1090-1153), Abbot of Clairvaux, claimed we should not be excessively curious about Christian beliefs, noting that humans are a vile dunghill.[8]

Christians who take this position find it easy to divide knowledge into two distinct categories. Tim LaHaye writes, ". . . only two lines of reasoning permeate all of literature: biblical revelation (the wisdom of God) and the wisdom of man,"[9] concluding our difficulties over the many centuries are due to fallible human reasoning. William Kilpatrick puts the same belief a little differently when he writes, ". . . scholarship is often a hindrance to understanding what is really happening."[10]

This kind of categorical thinking overlooks the fact that scholarship is essential to understanding the Bible. The Bible must be translated, read, and interpreted, all of which depend on scholarship. How often has a parable taken on new meaning when the historical context is explained by those who have studied biblical times? The parable of the Good Samaritan gains power when we understand how the Jews hated the Samaritans. Understanding requires reasoning and scholarship, not a blank mind. It may be true, in a sense, that reason is the root of most human problems, but reason is unavoidable.

It is dangerous to assume interpreting Scripture does not require reason. In fact, any mental activity, including scriptural interpretation, requires thinking. When those in authority believe otherwise, less powerful people end up being harmed. Remember the scripturally based witch-burnings, the Crusades, the Spanish Inquisition, and the trial of Galileo discussed in Chapter 2. Christians need to be skilled at opening and closing their minds to allow for critical thinking seasoned with conviction. We cannot escape the need for critical thinking.

Using the Shield on the Battlefield of Ideas —————

Some Christians stand boldly on the battlefield of ideas, bearing their shields of critical thinking. They use their reasoning skills to please and better understand God. There are several distinguishing characteristics of Christian critical thinkers.

74

Critical thinkers allow healthy doubt. James instructed his readers that "He who doubts is like a wave of the sea blown and tossed by the wind." (James 1:6b) This has been used by some to suggest Christians should not doubt issues of faith. But James' words are referring to petitioning God in prayer. When we ask God for wisdom to help us in times of trials and testings, we are to ask in faith, without any doubts, expecting we will receive wisdom. It is God's wisdom, as described in Proverbs, that will direct us in the way of righteousness and help us avoid the path of wickedness. Elsewhere, in a more general set of exhortations, Paul writes: "Test everything. Hold on to the good. Avoid every kind of evil." (1 Thessalonians 5:21, 22) Jesus is a great example of one who tested everything. He broke the religious leaders' stilted rules and challenged empty traditions.

Healthy doubt, when we hold firm to our convictions while questioning the evidence for our beliefs, is part of critical thinking. One characteristic of many Christian extremists is that they lack doubt. Proponents of positive thinking proclaim we can have anything if we think positively and raise our expectations. Some suggest the healthiest Christians are the wealthiest Christians. By overstating the power of positive thinking, they have lost their ability to doubt. They appear to have arrived at certainty, but certainty is an unlikely state. Christian author Daniel Taylor calls certainty a myth, noting with amazement the Christian leaders who proclaim their certainty, assuring listeners their doubts will disappear if they only believe.

Consider the television preacher and how fearfully he is made. I do not abuse him for being on television—it is the highest hill around. I do not complain that he asks for money—he has many barns to build. I allow him even his politics and prejudices (even as I wince when he makes them God's) because I have my politics and prejudices as well. But I do stand amazed at one thing. Where, someone tell me, did he get this brimming confidence? Not his confidence before men and women—the psychology of that I can understand—but this confidence before God. Did he talk to a burning bush? Why are there no signs of ashes on his head? Why does he seem unconcerned with such questions? Even "send me" Isaiah despaired of his unclean lips.[11]

75

Taylor describes what he calls a *reflective Christian*, a believer whose mind is active, curious, questioning, never at rest.

Taylor created an unscientific quiz to help his readers understand a reflective Christian. Although the questions are only partly serious, they allow us to see ourselves more clearly.

1. Are you, even after years of being a Christian, ever struck by the unlikelihood of the whole thing? Does one minute it seem perfectly natural and unquestionable that God exists and cares for the world, and the next moment uncommonly naive?

2. Do you ever think, "Those close to me would be shocked if they knew some of the doubts I have about my faith?" Do you ever scare even yourself with your doubts?

3. Have you sometimes felt like walking out of a church service because it seemed contrived and empty?

4. Have you ever felt intellectually embarrassed to admit that you were a Christian?

5. Do you ever feel somewhat schizophrenic about the relationship of your faith to the rest of your life? Do you find yourself compartmentalizing different aspects so that tensions between them are minimized?

6. If given a choice between sharing an island with Jerry Falwell and Phyllis Schlafly on the one hand, or Phil Donahue and Bella Abzug on the other, does one upset your stomach less than the other?[12]

It is a controversial set of questions. Those who don't doubt ask how one can be a Christian and doubt. Those of us with restless minds ask how can one be a Christian and not doubt. God can use nondoubters, and they often experience great peace in their faith. God can also use critical thinkers.

Psychologists recognize that not all minds operate the same way and have described different manners of thinking, called cognitive styles. For example, some people have a faster conceptual tempo, or decision-making speed, than others. The fast decision makers are called impulsive, and the slow decision makers, reflective. Fast decision makers prefer a fast answer even at the expense of sacrificing accuracy. Slow decision makers prefer accuracy but may take a long time in making decisions. Most of us have had the experience of going to lunch with a slow decision maker who spends twenty minutes looking at the menu. Of course most fall between the two extremes and have moderate decision-making rates, balancing accuracy and speed.

There are other interesting differences in cognitive style. Some people are better at ignoring distracting noise or movements than others; some are more likely to respond to a whole pattern, and others to pieces of a pattern; some rely on the environment for cues more than others, and so on.

Similarly, the ability to be certain, attributed to extremists and television evangelists, may be a particular cognitive style. The restless minds, those with opposing cognitive styles, may provide a nice balance to their certainty.

Balancing doubt and faith is difficult. Thomas was a man of faith, even called as a disciple of Christ, but he also had a restless mind. He was an empiricist, preferring firsthand experience to the word of others.

Now Thomas (called Didymus), one of the Twelve, was not with the disciples when Jesus came. When the other disciples told him that they had seen the Lord, he declared, "Unless I see the nail marks in his hands and put my finger where the nails were, and put my hand into his side, I will not believe it." A week later his disciples were in the house again, and Thomas was with them. Though the doors were locked, Jesus came and stood among them and said, "Peace be with you!" Then he said to Thomas, "Put your finger here; see my hands. Reach out your hand and put it into my side. Stop doubting and believe." Thomas said to him, "My Lord and my God!" Then Jesus told him, "Because you have seen me, you have believed; blessed are those who have not seen and yet have believed." (John 20:24-29)

77

Although he didn't condemn Thomas for his doubt, Jesus made it clear that faith exists in the absence of certainty. Christians who think critically doubt and test what they hear, but they realize the need to exercise faith.

Danish philosopher Soren Kierkegaard believed we need to reason things as far as possible and then make a leap of faith. It is impossible to reduce the Virgin Birth or the Resurrection to pure reason. We need faith. Doubt has an important place in Christians' minds, but it must coexist with faith.

Critical thinkers are skeptical. The Amazing Randi is a professional magician who specializes in debunking the claims of various spiritualists, mediums, and others who claim to perform mystical acts. Like Houdini before him, The Amazing Randi is a professional skeptic. Houdini had a strong interest in psychic abilities. He wanted to believe psychic powers were real, yet he tempered his desire with skepticism. As a professional magician, Houdini knew how easy it was to fool people. No one was able to demonstrate an ability Houdini could not replicate. In a similar vein of skepticism Randi has a standing offer to pay anyone $10,000 who can demonstrate psychic phenomena. He carries the check in his pocket where it has remained for years. No one has collected the offer. Like the offers made by *Scientific American*, no one has stepped forward who can demonstrate psychic powers under controlled conditions.

A common claim of psychics is that they can see an aura around people. Randi has asked these psychics if they can see an aura around him. Many claim they can. After putting a magazine in front of his face he asks if they can still see the aura. Most report they still can. "So," Randi will continue, "if I stepped behind a wall just tall enough to cover my head you should be able to tell where I am behind the wall?" No psychic has taken this challenge.

Skepticism is the willingness to withhold judgment. Most people are more skeptical in some areas than others. When a sales representative shows up at the door claiming a once-in-a-lifetime low price on a product, most of us are wisely skeptical. When fighting children claim, "He started it," or, "It was all her fault," it is natural to be skeptical. But when a Christian leader points a finger at the toys our children play with, claiming they are satanic, it is difficult for many to withhold judgment and maintain healthy skepticism.

Dr. Kenneth Kinghorn writes a column for *The Asbury Herald* in which he answers questions on Christian issues from readers. The following question was submitted by a troubled pastor:

> Some members of our congregation recently attended the meetings of an evangelist who preached in our area. He

insisted that children's Care Bears are satanic, and he demanded that parents collect all such toys belonging to their children and burn them. This issue is causing a great deal of confusion and worry, especially among recently converted young couples in our church. I don't want any of the children to suffer emotional harm from this turmoil. Should parents burn their children's Care Bears? What do you advise me to tell these couples?[13]

This letter shows the persuasive ability of Christian extremists. The members of this congregation were debating whether they should burn their childrens' toys because of the extreme views of one evangelist. Especially troubling is the reference to the recently converted couples in the church. Recent converts are often more authority-oriented than more experienced Christians who have learned to be skeptical.

This letter also shows the value of skepticism. Writing back, Dr. Kinghorn demonstrates the pastor's skepticism and a healthy fear of invalidity. He knew his opinion would have far-reaching consequences when he wrote, "I don't want any of the children to suffer emotional harm from this turmoil." The inquiring pastor's skepticism also kept him from making a snap judgment and from falling victim to groupthink. His skepticism also allowed him to hear this reply before he made his decision:

I would not recommend that parents or pastors confiscate children's Care Bears and burn or otherwise destroy them. An over-reaction to a possible danger could be just as bad as doing nothing. E. Stanley Jones liked to remind us, "What gets your attention, gets you." And too great a stress on the dark side of things creates fear—in the parents and the children alike. As I said, in themselves, Care Bears are not evil.

I do advise parents to take the time to monitor and supervise the moral development of their children and lead them in the ways of the Lord . . . . So long as a child considers his or her Care Bear as a make-believe friend, I don't see any objection to playing with Care Bears. But let's steer our children away from assigning magic or spiritual qualities to any object other than God. We can teach them about a real friend who has supernatural powers.[14]

Dr. Kinghorn's reply gave a different perspective than the one presented by the evangelist. The troubled pastor now has two perspectives on the same issue. This skeptical pastor probably also consulted other pastors and the leaders in his church, discussed it with his friends and family, read his Bible, and prayed about the issue. The result of his skepticism was information gathering. His scholarship made him better able to give good advice to his congregation.

Skepticism, like doubt, is not the absence of belief. Permanent indecision is at least as dangerous as premature judgment. Skepticism is a temporary state, allowing one to gather information for a good decision. Skepticism allows us to broaden our information base, seek out fresh perspectives, and avoid premature decisions.

Critical thinkers recognize cognitive traps. In their efforts to persuade, many unintentionally resort to faulty ways of thinking. Critical thinkers recognize these traps and increase their skepticism in response. In addition to the traps of vivid anecdotes, self-justification, correlation error, freezethink, and groupthink, consider a few other examples of cognitive traps.

1. *Dichotomous thinking or faulty dilemma.* Some extremists force their points by claiming there are only two alternatives. "Either you are for us or you are against us." This all-or-none thinking can be seen among those promoting positive thinking for Christians. Robert Schuller has suggested there are two kinds of people — those who see possibilities and those who do not. Although this provides powerful rhetoric for his possibility thinking, it is rarely accurate to reduce humans to two categories. It seems likely that some see possibilities in some situations but not in others.

Dichotomous thinking (sometimes called faulty dilemma) is also evident when Dave Hunt and T. A. McMahon imply that seminaries have lost their credibility by adding psychology courses to their curricula. Even if one accepts their arguments against psychology, is it reasonable to assume these seminaries are less qualified to teach traditional seminary courses than they were formerly?

When fund raisers push a collection can under your nose and ask, "Do you want to help starving children?" they are implying that if you don't donate you don't care about starving children. Things are never that simple, and there are many ways to help the hungry besides donating on street corners. The fund-raising efforts of some television evangelists also appeal to dichotomous thinking. The message is strong: If you support God's work then you will send your money to this ministry. The unspoken implication is that if you don't send money, then you don't support God's work. Some support these ministries simply to prevent feeling guilty and insensitive.

2. *Misuse of authority.* Often authors will imply authority for their positions by quoting those with similar persuasions. It is good to know that others agree, but such quotes only give one more opinion. Most of us can find two or three others who agree with us even if our ideas are filled with fallacy.

Watch for powerful words as a potential sign for the misuse of authority. *Research* is a widely used word with diverse meanings. Because of the status of science in today's society, referring to research can create an artificial respect for an author's positions. Research predicted Alf Landon to beat Franklin D. Roosevelt by a landslide in the 1936 presidential elections. *Literary Digest* sent out ten million postcards to Americans in a pre-election poll. Of the two million returned, a vast majority preferred Landon. Roosevelt won by a landslide despite the predicted results. The problem was with the method of selecting the sample. *Literary Digest* obtained the names for the survey from telephone listings and car registrations. Those who couldn't afford phones or cars were not surveyed, biasing the results.

81

Don't accept a hasty generalization — that is, basing a general statement on too small a sample. Imagine reading this message, "Research demonstrates that one person in three has had sex in a public place and sixty percent of Americans have had sex with two different partners within a 24-hour period." Before assuming these numbers are factual, consider that the survey sampled only *Playboy* readers. Knowing something about the research helps us think critically before coming to unreasonable conclusions. The adage is, "Analyze the proof before accepting the conclusion."

Don't accept the notion that only those in authority have the facts. Examine this statement from *Beyond Seduction*: "It takes a simple but firm decision based upon the facts to exchange the self-life for the Christ-life."[15] By the author implying he has the facts and others do not, he misuses his authority.

Beware of the misuse of Scripture. Misquoting Scripture or using Scripture out of context to prove a point is a misuse of authority. Because we believe the Bible to have authority, we should exercise care with attention to detail. Consider the following passage from 2 Timothy, used in *Seduction of Christianity* to argue against self-esteem.

> But mark this: There will be terrible times in the last days. People will be lovers of themselves, lovers of money, boastful, proud, abusive, disobedient to their parents, ungrateful, unholy, without love, unforgiving, slanderous, without self-control, brutal, not lovers of the good, treacherous, rash, conceited, lovers of pleasure rather than lovers of God... (2 Timothy 3:1-4).

It seems unlikely Paul was arguing against self-esteem in this passage. Paul is describing the vices that will characterize people in the last days of this age, before the Second Coming. Even Paul's description that "People will be lovers of themselves" does not mean they will have self-esteem. It just means that they will be selfish. Later in the same list he mentions those who oppose the truth and violate women. Moreover, Paul's conclusion is that these deceivers won't get very far because their folly will be clear to all. Self-esteem is not what Paul is addressing in this passage, and yet it is used to add credibility to Hunt and McMahon's arguments against self-esteem.

3. *Poisoning the wells.* Elbert Hubbard once wrote, "If you can't answer a man's arguments, all is not lost. You can still call him vile names." This logical trick occurs when a person is discredited by name-calling. As a consequence, that person's evidence is then considered unreliable. When reading Christian authors who refer to humanists as "leeches who live off the government," the well has already been poisoned before the argument has begun.

Confronting faulty logic is important, but attacking the character of opponents has no connection to the integrity of an

82

argument. Paul instructed the Colossians: "Be wise in the way you act toward outsiders; make the most of every opportunity. Let your conversation be always full of grace, seasoned with salt, so that you may know how to answer everyone." (Colossians 4:5, 6) It requires balance to confront error, seasoning our speech with salt, while being gracious to others. As Christians, let's help purify the well.

4. *Hasty generalizations.* Critical thinkers watch for overgeneralizations. We sometimes read statements such as "Women approach the world with their emotions," or "Homosexuals have a strong interest in art." These generalizations show that the authors jumped to conclusions. Women, like men, approach the world in a variety of ways. Some homosexuals like football and not art.

When one critic of psychology writes, "There is no emotional problem that psychology attempts to deal with for which the Bible does not claim that God Himself offers a complete cure,"[16] he uses a hasty generalization. What about biofeedback and stress management techniques for pain control? What about psychotherapy for panic attacks? What about cognitive rehabilitation for those with brain damage? By recognizing and avoiding cognitive traps, critical thinkers are better able to seek truth.

Christian critical thinkers seek God's guidance. Christians have extra resources to cope with the battlefield of ideas. Through prayer, careful Bible study, the fellowship and wisdom of other believers, worship, and inspirational reading, we can use our minds to understand God and His world.

Some believers have used God's direction to confront prevailing standards even when others have been caught up in the groupthink of the day. A few insightful Christians maintained a strong testimony against slavery in the days when many supported slavery with Bible passages. Other Christians have had prophetic roles in speaking against evil social policies, including racial injustices. Christians seeking God's guidance above popular teachings, theories, and opinions can honor and serve Him with their critical thinking.

CHAPTER SIX

The Power Of the Mind

The pink cover of Norman Vincent Peale's *The Power of Positive Thinking* brightens any bookshelf. The cover boasts of three million copies sold and boldly describes the book as "the greatest inspirational bestseller of our time." On the back, Peale explains why he wrote the book: "This book is written with the sole objective of helping the reader achieve a happy, satisfying, and worthwhile life."

Equally flamboyant is a purple volume, *The Seduction of Christianity*, written by Dave Hunt and T. A. McMahon. The cover clashes with Peale's pink book and so do the ideas. The subtitle is *Spiritual Discernment in the Last Days*. A warning by the authors on the back cover states that the seduction of Christianity will not appear as a frontal attack on our faith but as "fashionable philosophies" offering to make us happier, healthier, and more spiritual.

One book cover claims that positive thinking can be used to "break the worry habit, get other people to like you, and energize your life." The other book's cover states there are dangers in the growing practice of positive and possibility thinking. One cover promises a fuller life and satisfying success while the other warns of a "new worldview more subtle and more seductive than anything the world has ever experienced." Both books claim to have the best spiritual interests of the reader at heart.

It is clear that positive thinking is having a major impact on current evangelicalism, despite the crossfire. Robert Schuller, Paul Yonggi Cho, and other pastors and authors of prominence have joined Peale in promoting the power of positive thinking. And the positive thinking advocates have some points worth considering. Yet Dave Hunt, T. A. McMahon, and other critics insist positive thinking is wrong, that its proponents have infused evil and misleading beliefs into their doctrine.

Facing such obvious disagreement, both sides have been guilty of unfounded generalizations about the opposing side. The advocates of positive thinking have assumed that since positive thinking is useful in some situations it is useful in all. The opponents claim there are defects in the basis of positive thinking and therefore, there can't be any value in its use. The opponents rashly conclude that all positive thinking is evil, while the other side impulsively embraces positive thinking as a central theme of the Christian faith. Authors on both sides state their positions with fervor and certainty, often creating confusion among evangelical readers. The following letter appeared in the October 1986 issue of *Evangelical Friend* magazine:

> When the July / August *Evangelical Friend* came I was reading *The Seduction of Christianity* by Dave Hunt and T. A. McMahon. I read the news item . . . about Dr. Cho's Korean Church and thought, *now that seems like he's winning souls for Jesus Christ.* But what did I just read about Cho in this book? "Cho teaches that positive thinking, positive speaking, and positive visualizing are the keys to success. Anyone can 'incubate' and give birth to physical reality by creating a vivid image in his or her mind and focusing upon it." After reading the article in *Evangelical Friend*, most people would think he is doing great works for the Lord, but that is not true. Please read *The Seduction of Christianity.*

86

For those impressed by numbers and comparisons, it is noted that Cho's Presbyterian Church in Seoul, Korea, with 400,000 members is the largest Christian church in the world. And with the largest audience in the world of any religious television program, *The Hour of Power*, Dr. Robert Schuller's positive thinking doctrine is heard by over two million viewers each week. Even Hunt acknowledges that Cho "almost always presents excellent Bible teaching," but notes it is "sometimes unfortunately mixed with the occult ideas of visualization and mind-power." Possibility thinkers are given a doctrine of hope that offers the promise that dreams and wishes will be realized if they think right and act right.

Are promoters of positive thinking betraying biblical Christianity? Are they allowing Satan a foothold in the evangelical community? Is positive thinking an acceptable practice for Christians, or is it, as Hunt and McMahon suggest, full of fallacy and seduction? These are questions Christians are challenged to confront—challenges that demand critical thinking. Somewhere in the crossfire of ideas is truth. The following questions are a guide through the crossfire. But remember, this guide needs to be looked at just as critically as the claims examined.

Question 1: Does Positive Thinking Have a Spiritual Dimension?

Both the advocates and the critics of positive thinking are quick to point to its spiritual implications. Advocates see positive thinking as a spiritual tool, whereas critics see it as spiritually dangerous. Peale summarizes positive thinking this way:

> Whatever your situation may be, you can improve it. First, quiet your mind so that inspirations may rise from its depth. Believe that God is now helping you. Visualize achievement. Organize your life on a spiritual basis so that God's principles work within you. Hold firmly in your mind a picture not of failure but of success. Do these things and creative thought will flow freely from your mind. This is an amazing law, one that can change anybody's life including your own. An inflow of new thoughts can remake you regardless of every difficulty you may now face, and I repeat—*every difficulty*.[1]

Notice that Peale's positive thinking focuses on human accomplishment rather than godliness. It might even be perceived as a mechanism to force God to do our will. This is one of Hunt and McMahon's objections to the tenets of positive mental attitude (PMA). They write of those believing PMA doctrines, ". . . to them faith is not placed *in* God but is a power directed at God, which forces Him to do for us what we have believed He will do." But also notice that Peale's positive thinking leaves room for God's influence in our lives. One page after the preceding quote in Peale's book, he reports an instance of witnessing God's truth to a friend who "became an enthusiastic practicing follower of Jesus Christ. Through real faith and a

87

complete change of thoughts and personal habits, wrong thinking and wrong acting were removed from his nature." Thus, Peale does not deny right and wrong or advocate a life without godly faith.

In the same way, Robert Schuller advocates a spiritual dimension to his possibility thinking. Schuller endorses the power of Jesus Christ and the need to draw on His strength and vitality. The following prayer is printed in one of his books:

> Jesus Christ, come into my life. Flush all sins out of my spirit. Love people through me. I believe you are coming into me now in the form of God-filled ideas. I know I have enormous undiscovered, untapped energy within me. I feel young, I have energy, I am energetic. Thank you for this vitality and strength of mind and body. Live within me, O God, and do good works now through me. Thank you again. Amen.[2]

Though Peale's and Schuller's PMA teachings may make us uncomfortable because they minimize traditional teachings of human depravity, both authors recognize the personal presence and power of God as an essential element of Christian doctrine. Peale writes:

> This is one of the simplest teachings in religion, namely, that Almighty God will be your companion, will stand by you, help you, and see you through. No other idea is so powerful in developing self-confidence as this simple belief when practiced.[3]

88 Although Peale uses this doctrine to promote personal success and well-being, the writer of Hebrews uses a similar argument to promote contentedness. Both suggest the presence of God can drive away fear and promote confidence.

> Keep your lives free from the love of money and be content with what you have, because God has said, "Never will I leave you; never will I forsake you." So we say with confidence, "The Lord is my helper; I will not be afraid. What can man do to me?" (Hebrews 13:5-6)

It is the Christianizing of positive thinking that concerns critics of PMA. Because Peale, Schuller, Cho, and others have mixed biblical truth with what Hunt and McMahon consider a pagan and occult technique (PMA), they have allegedly seduced Christians away from the basics of the faith.

Advocates and critics of positive thinking agree that it can have a spiritual dimension. Some would say PMA enhances our understanding of God's presence in our life while others say it pollutes Christianity and leads us to an unhealthy understanding of God.

Question 2: Is There Power in the Mind? _____

In a study mentioned briefly in Chapter 3, psychologist Robert Rosenthal assigned one hundred airmen to one of five math classes. Their teachers, who were unaware the students were randomly assigned, were told the students had been selected for their classes based on their levels of ability. Surprisingly, students in the "high-ability" classes improved more than those in the "low-ability" classes even though their initial abilities were the same. The only difference between the students was in the minds of the teachers. The beliefs of the teachers somehow affected what took place in the classroom. Students performed as they were expected to perform. Certainly there is power in the mind, especially when it affects the way we treat others.

Similarly, those who believe they control their own future achieve more and are better able to deal with their problems than those who believe their future depends on factors beyond their control. Self-confidence is a predictor of success. Conversely, those who believe they are helpless and have no control over their environment tend to be more depressed and less successful than others.

89

The power of thinking is demonstrated in the life of John, a man who experienced panic attacks almost every day. During the attacks his heart raced, he was short of breath, and he imagined he was dying or going crazy. After his first session in psychotherapy, John never again had a full-blown panic attack because of a simple assignment. He was told to deliberately have a panic attack. It sounds too easy, but those with panic attacks often have great anxiety about having another panic attack. The more they think, "Oh no! I'm about to have a panic attack," the more anxious they feel. The more anxious they feel, the more likely they are to have a panic attack. By assigning John the task of having a panic attack, his vicious cycle was broken and most of the anxiety ceased. By reducing the fear, he made himself unable to have another attack. John lacked confidence and constantly saw himself as weak and fragile before therapy. After six months of therapy, he saw himself in control of his emotions, able to prevent panic attacks by managing his thoughts. Of course John is only one person and this is a vivid anecdote. But psychotherapy researchers are reporting similar results with large groups of clients with panic disorder—evidence there is power in the mind.

But the mind does not contain limitless power. Grocery store aisles are stocked with products claiming to use subliminal messages. By listening to tapes of ocean waves (with subliminal audible messages being given at the same time), one can supposedly stop smoking, reduce eating, and manage stress better. Controlled laboratory studies of the effectiveness of subliminal messages have consistently shown them to be ineffective, yet the idea of a powerful key to the mind through the unconscious continues to be popularly accepted.

The popular fascination with subliminal messages started in a New Jersey movie theater in the late 1950s. During the movie, the words "Eat popcorn" and "Drink Coca-Cola" were flashed on the screen so quickly that they could not be consciously perceived. The theater used the messages for six weeks and claimed their concession sales increased dramatically. But the theater failed to take into account the weather conditions (people drink more when it's hot) and the films shown during the six weeks (exciting movies sell more popcorn). Subsequent studies that considered these factors demonstrated subliminal messages to be ineffective. In spite of this evidence, some advertisers continue to use this technique. However, they would have better results if they announced their message loudly and clearly rather than subliminally.

The subliminal message myth has infiltrated Christian markets as well. A Christian radio station advertises "Christian weight loss" products, one of which claimed that rapid weight loss can result by using a tape with subliminal messages and a skin patch with four minerals and two herbs! Christianizing a myth does not make the myth true.

Customers will be disappointed if they buy those subliminal weight loss tapes at the local supermarket and so will Christians who respond to the radio ad for a similar product. Those who buy these products won't lose weight by using the tapes, not because the mind isn't powerful, but because the mind is not powerful in the way these tapes suggest.

Question 3: Is the Bible Positive or Negative? _____

In the sequel to *Seduction of Christianity*, the author, Mr. Hunt, notes that advocates of PMA believe the Bible to be the most positive book in the world. Hunt objects, noting that neither the word "positive" nor the the word "mental" appears in the Bible. But critical thinking suggests that the presence or absence of certain English words, which themselves are subject to correct translation, should not be used to argue the substance of God's Word. The word "Trinity" doesn't appear either, but the Bible certainly supports the doctrine of a triune God.

Hunt has some stronger arguments against the Bible being a PMA textbook. He notes the numerous biblical examples of those who professed their own powerlessness before calling on God's strength. When Isaiah stood in the presence of the Lord, he was humbled and cried, "Woe is me, for I am ruined! Because I am a man of unclean lips, and I live among a people of unclean lips; for my eyes have seen the King, the Lord of hosts." (Isaiah 6:5) Moreover, it is not difficult to find accounts of Jesus dealing quite negatively with people. He accused the Pharisees of being whitewashed tombs and spoke *91* forthrightly about their hypocrisy.

But we can also argue that the Bible is quite positive. The Old Testament speaks of our unworthy condition before God, and the New Testament gives hope through the atoning work of Jesus Christ. We, like Simeon as he held the infant Jesus, believe we have seen our salvation in Jesus. And we, like the Prodigal Son, were lost but have now been found. Even passages about church discipline need to be seen in the positive context of Christian acceptance, forgiveness, and renewal. Of all books, the Bible is a book of comfort and hope. It is a positive book.

Even if we conclude the Bible's message is generally positive, we cannot infer that the Bible promotes achievement and personal success. This is a separate issue. Hunt and McMahon are right when they argue we should not view God as our genie who will give us whatever we want if we properly tap into His power. The Bible is God's written disclosure of Himself to us. Where human reasoning and help are weak and fade away, God's Word never fails. "The grass withers and the flowers fall, but the word of the Lord stands forever." (1 Peter 1:24b, 25)

Advocates of PMA are correct when they point out that the Bible is a positive book. But Hunt and McMahon wisely caution that the Bible is not designed to help us accomplish personal goals. Proponents and critics of Christian positive thinking are both right—and both wrong. Critical thinking helps us to identify truth in each set of claims.

Question 4: Is There any Middle Ground? _____

As her family pulled out of a gas station, a five-year-old noted that there are two kinds of gas. Since she was beginning to read, her father assumed she had noticed the labels on the gas pumps and was referring to "regular" and "unleaded."

"Yes", he answered, "there are two kinds of gas."

"The car kind and the people kind," she replied.

This five-year-old, one of our daughters, was using her abilities of categorization to come to her unintentionally humorous conclusion. Throughout life we use categories to help us think about certain issues. Her categories were fine, but there are more than two kinds of gas. She omitted other valid categories by using dichotomous thinking. She hadn't thought about natural gas (methane, that is, not the people kind!), propane gas, steam, and other forms of gas.

Authors on both sides of the PMA debate have also resorted to dichotomous thinking in their writings. Robert Schuller writes:

> There are two basic types of thinkers within the human family. I choose to call these two types "possibility thinkers" and "impossibility thinkers." Which kind are you? . . . Impossibility thinkers are people who make swift, sweeping passes over a proposed idea, scanning it

92

with a sharp negative eye, looking only for the distasteful aspects. . . . The possibility thinkers perceptively probe every problem, proposal, and opportunity to discover the positive aspects present in almost every human situation.[4]

Although Schuller is making a useful point, he is seeing things in all-or-nothing terms. He implies that impossibility thinking always fails and possibility thinking "often wins over impossible odds." Surely there are many who see possibilities in some situations and see impossibilities in others. Schuller leaves no room for middle ground.

Norman Vincent Peale also uses dichotomous thinking in his description of positive thinkers.

If you or I or anybody think constantly of the forces that seem to be against us, we will build them up into a power far beyond that which is justified. They will assume a formidable strength which they do not actually possess. But if, on the contrary, you mentally visualize and affirm and reaffirm your assets and keep your thoughts on them, emphasizing them to the fullest extent, you will rise out of any difficulty regardless of what it may be. Your inner powers will reassert themselves and, with the help of God, lift you from defeat to victory.[5]

Peale is suggesting positive thinking will deliver one from any difficulty and that negative thinking will be oppressive. Many tragic situations will never be resolved by positive thinking.

The critics of PMA are also guilty of using dichotomous thinking. They believe that in PMA there are errors, weaknesses, or elements of incompatibility with Scripture. Dave Hunt calls PMA a "secular counterfeit," implying one must completely reject the teachings of PMA in order to maintain a biblical Christian faith. He identifies PMA with New Age religion, Eastern heresy, and a satanic influence in the church. Consequently, everything about PMA must be rejected because there is not one iota of truth in it. This is an easy mistake to make when it appears at first glance that there are only two alternatives, to accept or reject. It is the lazy way to consider an issue. Critical thinkers will consider the complexity of an issue, knowing that many things in life cannot be crowded into an either/or proposition.

93

In spite of the charges that they are offering a "secular counterfeit," Dr. Schuller's and Dr. Peale's ministries have been helpful to tens of thousands of Christians. Many testify that Schuller's and Peale's ministries have led them to an orthodox Christian faith.

After reading *The Seduction of Christianity* and *Beyond Seduction*, one might expect Robert Schuller's books to be filled with overt heresy and an unrealistic emphasis on personal success and prosperity. Contrary to those expectations, it is surprising to read:

> The most tragic blind spot in any personal philosophy of life is the concept that "If I'm greedy I'll get ahead." Nothing could be further from the truth. "Whatever a man sows, that shall he also reap." (see Galatians 6:7)[6]

We are called to look for truth. Schuller and Peale have found some truth. Hunt and McMahon have found some truth. But dichotomous thinking is an inadequate tool in the search for truth.

Question 5: Is There Value in Thinking Positively? —————

Peale writes, "If you or I or anybody think constantly of the forces that seem to be against us, we will build them up into a power far beyond that which is justified."[7] Clinical experience in working with hundreds of depressed and anxious clients, many of whom are Christians, supports Peale's assertion. Distorted thinking and negative thoughts lead to frustration, anger, and dysphoria. Positive thinking can have the opposite effect—leading to renewed enthusiasm, happiness, and motivation.

A *New York Times* article tells a fascinating story of a bus driver who greeted his passengers by asking them not to smile. As each rider entered, the driver said, "No smiling, please!" The reaction was predictable. Riders began smiling, even those with the sourest dispositions. They enjoyed watching new riders as they entered the bus, and they told others to "Have a nice day" as they left the bus. By using a paradoxical strategy, the bus driver had his passengers thinking positive, good thoughts rather than the typical anxiety-filled thoughts of a New York City morning. The smile was infectious.

Is positive thinking un-Christian? Peace and joy are undeniable aspects of New Testament Christianity. Peale writes that the "chief struggle . . . in gaining mental peace is the effort of revamping your thinking to the relaxed attitude of acceptance of God's gift of peace."[8] Maybe we need to devote more energy to finding personal peace before God. Peale's mechanism of changing our thinking is a useful way of finding peace.

The message of the Gospel changes our thinking from negative to positive. In the seventh chapter of Romans, Paul described the cognitive turmoil he experienced over sin. Even though he wanted to do right, he often found himself doing wrong. After expressing the negative (but realistic) thoughts about the futility of sin, Paul summarized the gospel message by proclaiming:

> Thanks be to God—through Jesus Christ our Lord! So then, I myself in my mind am a slave to God's law, but in the sinful nature a slave to the law of sin. Therefore, there is now no condemnation for those who are in Christ Jesus, because through Christ Jesus the law of the Spirit of life set me free from the law of sin and death. (Romans 7:25-8:2)

The gospel message allows us to exchange the negative thoughts of our inadequacy for the positive thoughts of Christ's sufficiency. There is hope and peace and encouragement in the "law of the Spirit of life in Christ Jesus." (Romans 8:2) Even if Peale's terminology and theological emphases vary from what one is accustomed to, the essence of positive thinking can be found in the Gospel. **95**

Some criticize Schuller and Peale because PMA is filled with ambition. Schuller's story of building the Crystal Cathedral and its congregation is a story of ambition. Is ambition compatible with Christianity? In an excellent article, John Throop notes that ambition can "reveal a God who made us in his creative and dynamic image," that ambition can be experienced in cooperation with others toward a noble goal, and that it can be present simultaneously with servanthood.[9] The Bible speaks against "selfish ambition," but not all ambition is selfish.

Another consideration is whether or not faith in oneself precludes faith in God. Hunt writes, "True faith rests in God's love and care, relieving us of every burden and producing 'the peace of God which passeth all understanding'. (Philippians 4:7) The secular counterfeit of faith is called a 'positive mental attitude'."[10] Is this a necessary distinction? If we have faith in God must we abandon positive attitudes and faith in ourselves? The Apostle Paul frequently instructed his readers to follow his example. He had faith in God but he also had confidence he was living a consistent Christian life. He had faith in God first and faith in himself second. Self-confidence and ambition do not necessarily preclude faith in God. God calls us to be bold and zealous in our faith, requiring self-confidence and faith in ourselves.

Even if Schuller and Peale are wrong on some points, their writings can still be valuable and instructive on other points. Many have found the love of Christ through their ministries.

Critical Thinking about Positive Thinking

Positive thinking can be frightening because in extreme forms it can lead us away from valuing the things God would have us value. Dave Hunt tells the story of a Jewish friend who asked a Christian why he should believe in Christianity.

> "Because you'll be happy. Jesus will give you happiness."
> "But I'm already happy," he told the Christian.
> "Yes, but Jesus will make you healthier."
> "But I'm already healthy," the Jew replied.
> "He can make you wealthier," the Christian said.[11]

This is an example of extreme positive thinking. The Bible does not support the conclusion that God wants us rich. But not all positive thinking goes this far.

A form of psychotherapy, called cognitive therapy, emphasizes the use of thinking skills to feel better. Clients are taught to abandon old destructive ways of thinking and employ more accurate ways of thinking. Sometimes clients think too optimistically, and they need to be more realistic. Other times they think too pessimistically and need to be more optimistic.

Several things can be learned from cognitive therapy. First, we tend to see the worst in situations. One of us (Mark) was humbled by this tendency over a relatively minor incident.

I received a notice from my home mortgage carrier informing me that I had neglected to respond to a request for insurance information, a request I had no recollection of receiving. Because I had failed to respond they were going to add $1,192 to my mortgage amount. That's an expensive insurance policy for a three-bedroom house! I was irritable with my family all evening and lay awake most of the night worrying about this notice. Early the next morning I called to check it out. "We're sorry about that notice," came the voice on the other end of the phone. "That was sent out in error. All we need is your social security number." I had wasted an evening of my life worrying for no reason. I saw the worst in the situation.

We've all heard of Murphy's Law — if something bad can happen, it will. Of course Murphy's law is false, but it often seems true. Someone has offered several creative and humorous corollaries to Murphy's law:

A $300.00 picture tube will protect a 10 cent fuse by blowing first.
The other line always moves faster.
A bird in hand is safer than one overhead.
The shortest distance between any two points is under construction.
Everything east of the San Andreas fault will eventually plunge into the Atlantic Ocean.

The corollaries are just as false as Murphy's Law, but they sometimes seem true because we tend to see the worst in situations. When we assume the worst, we feel depressed and sad and anxious and angry. Sometimes those feelings are caused by distorted thinking, as they were after the mistaken insurance notice. Thinking more positively is appropriate in such situations.

Second, blind optimism is rarely appropriate. Havelock Ellis, an English psychologist and author, wrote, "The place where optimism most flourishes is the lunatic asylum."[12] Positive thinking can easily go too far. All things are not possible regardless of how positively one thinks. The child from

Harlem will probably not become president of IBM, no matter how positively he or she thinks, because opportunity is not limitless.

The children's book based on Walt Disney's *Dumbo* concludes with the other elephants all trying to learn to fly. But the story ends by saying that the elephants never learned to fly because "they did not know Dumbo's secret." And what was the secret? The secret was to believe in yourself. But this advice overlooked reality. The other elephants could believe in themselves just as strongly as Dumbo, but without those gigantic ears they could never fly. When positive thinking goes to the point of blind optimism, it sets the believer up for failure.

Mike was a positive thinker. Even after his wife's cancer had spread to her liver, he was sure she would be successfully treated with chemotherapy. Conversations with Mike's physician suggested he was using denial. His wife was terminally ill, and he refused to admit it. Mike felt disbelief and despair when his wife finally died. His positive thinking had failed. How much better it would have been if Mike could have been realistic instead of optimistic.

Poet Alexander Pope, in a 1727 letter, wrote, "Life's greatest disappointments, as well as its highest achievements are born of the most positive expectations."[13] By thinking positively and self-confidently we can set ourselves up for a great fall when we fail. In the comic strip *Peanuts*, Charlie Brown's friend Linus once said, "There's no heavier burden than a great potential." Positive thinking, especially when excessively optimistic, is dangerous.

Third, we all tend to have a selfish bias in our thinking. David Myers and Malcolm Jeeves identify eight ways we tend toward self-centered biases.

1. We tend to accept more responsibility for our successes than our failures.
2. We tend to see ourselves as better than average on some traits, such as intelligence.
3. We accept flattering descriptions of ourselves as more valid than critical descriptions.
4. We distort our memories of the past to enhance our views of ourselves.

5. We justify our harmful actions by finding good reasons for doing them.
6. We overestimate the accuracy of our beliefs and opinions.
7. We remember pleasant events more than unpleasant ones and are unrealistically optimistic about the future.
8. We overestimate our ability to resist evil.[14]

The blind spot of the positive thinking and human potential movements is that we are already unrealistically self-centered in our views of the world. Encouraging some people to think more positively about themselves may make the self-centered bias even worse. In the process, we might miss the potential for evil and destruction that clearly infects our species. Our natural human tendencies make some positive thinking unnecessary.

There is power in the mind and there are benefits of thinking positively. But there are also problems with positive thinking.

CHAPTER SEVEN

Is Psychology Seducing Christianity?

Mornings are bleak for Sharon. At the end of a restless night she'll lie in bed staring at the ceiling until her eyes blur, her mind filled with the dread of another day. Routine household chores have become monumental tasks and formerly appetizing foods have lost all appeal. The joy of her new son, now six-months old, has been overshadowed by self-doubt and sorrow that seems almost unbearable. Her sense of aloneness is not lessened by the presence of others. Guilt and self-condemnation are part of her daily routine. She thinks endlessly about her failures as a mother and as a Christian.[1]

Sharon is suffering the classic symptoms of depression: sleep changes, loss of appetite, motivational deficits, inaccurate self-image, self-condemnation, and pervasive sadness. Her symptoms began shortly after she gave birth to her first child. Giving up her successful career to shape the life of a newborn seemed a small price to pay at the time. But now she wonders if she has anything to offer her son.

Counseling with her pastor has helped in recent months, *101* but signs of progress have been overshadowed by ominous emotions that remain. Her pastor, concerned that Sharon has not improved more rapidly, recently recommended Sharon get professional help for her depression. With that suggestion, a new emotional dilemma was created for Sharon because she once read several fascinating books about psychology. According to the authors of these books, the mental health professions have seduced Christians and led millions away from scriptural teachings. Could it be that going to a professional psychologist would result in spiritual suicide? Is psychology humanistic, ineffective, and antibiblical as the critics claim?

The confusion that Sharon faces is commonly felt by Christians needing help. Christian criticism of psychology has generated a reverberating confusion about the clinical and scientific methods of psychology and created a fear that prevents many from seeking needed psychological help. Sharon needs critical thinking skills to make a good decision.

The critics of psychology, like the critics of positive thinking, are often respected and well meaning authors whose arguments must be considered carefully. But their writings sometimes omit perspectives that would foster a more balanced understanding of psychotherapy. Sharon's struggle, and that of many Christians in her situation, requires a critical evaluation of some important questions.

Does Psychology Advocate Self-glorification? _____

For the past fifty years psychologists have been interested in the self. "Self" psychologists, such as Carl Jung, Alfred Adler, Erich Fromm, Abraham Maslow, Gordon Allport, and Carl Rogers, have written about self-esteem, self-image, self-realization, and self-actualization. In his book, *Psychological Seduction*, William Kirk Kilpatrick identifies this emphasis as antithetical to Christian thought. Kilpatrick suggests that psychologists see self as the ultimate reality in life, ignoring concern for others and humanitarian compassion, resulting in a striving to be like God and an unhealthy pursuit of happiness. If Sharon does seek help from a psychologist she might, according to Kilpatrick, be led away from a Christian lifestyle and be trained to look out only for her own needs, minimizing her concern for others. In his second book, *The Emperor's New Clothes: The Naked Truth About the New Psychology*, Kilpatrick continues this theme by implying self psychologists have been silent on social issues and uninterested in the welfare of others.

102

In a similar but more extreme manner, Dave Hunt and T. A. McMahon have criticized psychology's use of self-concept in *The Seduction of Christianity*. They argue psychology's emphasis on self-esteem is contrary to the humility of Moses that God chose to reward (Numbers 12:3) and signifies the coming of the end times.

The concerns of Kilpatrick, Hunt, and McMahon must be taken seriously. Book titles such as *Looking Out for Number One* and *Pulling Your Own Strings* suggest psychologists have sometimes emphasized self to the exclusion of concern for others. Although many such books are less self-centered than the titles imply, in some popular psychological writings self-image and self-glorification, or narcissism, have been confused. Unfortunately, it appears that they may have also been confused by the critics of psychology.

Mainstream psychology's position on self-image can be clarified with the analogy of a marksman shooting at a target. A marksman is more concerned with accuracy than with whether the shot is low or high. Concepts of low or high are only used to improve accuracy. Never would a marksman conclude "the higher the better." Likewise, psychologists have traditionally been interested in accuracy of self-concept. It may be important to observe whether self-image is low or high, but only for the sake of adjusting accuracy. Few psychologists have concluded "the higher the better."

Classical self psychologists made a distinction between accurate self-image and the excessive self-love of narcissism. Allport wrote that inherent narcissism could not be dominant in the psychologically mature individual. Fromm, Adler, Maslow, Allport, and Rogers all emphasized that an individual with a healthy self-image is rarely selfish. Kilpatrick's perspective that self psychology has obscured a concern for others may be true of some popular psychological writings, but it does not represent mainstream psychology.

In addition to Kilpatrick's mistaken conclusion about what mainstream psychology believes a healthy self-image to be, Hunt and McMahon are also in error. They have confused self-image with narcissism. They note that Paul warned Timothy that in the last days "People will be lovers of themselves" (2 Timothy 3:2), which means selfish. But there is little doubt that Paul himself had a healthy self-image. He wrote frequently of his accomplishments and encouraged his readers to imitate him. But Paul was not narcissistic, focusing on himself to the exclusion of a concern for others. Moses also appeared to develop an accurate self-image as evidenced by his style of leadership. While humility and narcissism are incompatible,

103

humility and a healthy self-image are not. Humility involves self-acceptance. The person who has never learned to accept him or herself ends up spending large amounts of time thinking about inadequacies or failures. This self-absorption is not healthy and could be avoided with self-acceptance. Humility requires an accurate self-image that, in turn, requires a humble awareness of personal limitations.

Does psychology advocate self-glorification? Perhaps in some popular psychological writings, but the classical notion of self has been misunderstood by the critics of psychology. Narcissism is not the goal of traditional psychological treatment, realism is. Seeking to develop accurate self-image is very different from teaching self-glorification.

The goal of Christian maturity is to focus our attentions more and more upon God's character. This is impossible for the narcissist. It is also impossible for Sharon because her attentions are directed toward herself in self-condemnation. Unless her self-image can be restructured, she will be unable to focus on God's character. The therapeutic goal is not necessarily to raise her self-image, but rather to help her understand her view of herself and to facilitate greater accuracy of self-perception.

Is Psychology Humanism?

Portions of psychology have been influenced significantly by humanistic philosophies, and this has led some Christian critics to conclude that psychology is dangerous. Some even label it a competing religion. Paul Vitz, in his book, *Psychology as Religion: The Cult of Self Worship*,[2] argues that the religion of psychology has become a secular humanism. Kilpatrick echoes this in his writings when he states that he was very nearly converted to the faith of humanistic psychology but escaped before it was too late. Similarly, the *Bible-Science Newsletter* of February 1986 contains articles equating traditional psychology with secular humanism. These critics believe psychology is humanistic and a clear and present danger to Christians.

Is humanism really the enemy? Because of the emphasis on concern for the less fortunate, humanism has been viewed by some as having been an integral part of Christianity since the Renaissance. Humanists traditionally have been passionately involved in issues of social justice, concerns Christians share. Many other emphases of humanistic psychology are very similar to those of Christianity. For example, both emphasize social compassion for others in need, the merit of personal growth and responsibility, the value of suffering, the distinction between animal and human, and the importance of responsible decision making.

Being a Christian in a psychological era is often like walking a tightrope. If we lean too far to the left, we may become spiritually insensitive and begin to look to the human experience as the ultimate reality. Many of the leaders in psychology have done this. Sigmund Freud, Abraham Maslow, Carl Rogers (at one time), Albert Ellis, and many others have professed publicly that God is a human invention with psychological implications. In so doing, the power of God is neglected. An atheistic humanism is the result of this neglect, and it has had an influence on psychological thought. But if we lean too far to the right, we may miss much of God's truth revealed in sources other than Scripture. If Sharon concludes psychology is antibiblical, she will not get help for her depression despite the availability of relatively quick, effective psychological treatments that have no implicit atheistic assumptions. It is hasty to assume that all psychology is misguided because some of the leaders have been misguided. Walking on the tightrope requires great balance and constant assessment of one's position. It requires critical thinking.

Are the Methods Used by Psychologists Spiritually Dangerous?

105

Looking for a psychologist can be likened to shopping for toothpaste. One is immediately overwhelmed by the plethora of brand labels: psychoanalysis, behaviorism, client-centered therapy, cognitive restructuring, transactional analysis, gestalt therapy, and so on. To ask if psychotherapy is spiritually dangerous is like asking if toothpaste is white: It depends on the brand. Add to this the complication that all psychotherapies are delivered by a person with his or her own distinct spiritual values, which will influence the treatment. The possible combinations of values and therapies are endless! It is fruitless to attempt to decide whether all psychotherapy is spiritually dangerous. A better question for Sharon might be, Is this particular psychotherapy delivered by this therapist spiritually dangerous to me?

Regrettably, critics of psychology have often evaluated the spirituality of the discipline by investigating only a few of the available psychotherapies. In *The Psychological Way/The Spiritual Way*,[3] Martin and Deidre Bobgan describe the danger of psychological methods of treatment. The Bobgans raise some important objections to prevailing psychotherapeutic techniques, but most of their critique involves identifying the fringes of psychology and then condemning all psychology. If Sharon had recently read their book, she might anticipate that a psychologist would almost certainly use methods such as scream therapy, encounter groups, est, arica, and transcendental meditation. Having completed doctoral programs in psychology at major secular universities, it is interesting that neither of us have studied any of these techniques. In fact, we're not sure how to pronounce one of them! These techniques are rarely used by psychologists and referring to them when criticizing psychology is the equivalent of referring to astrology to criticize astronomers or using the *National Enquirer* to criticize journalists.

The Bobgans respond to this criticism by noting that they also criticized mainstream psychotherapeutic techniques. Their response to the material in this chapter was printed as a letter to the editor in the June 17, 1988, issue of *Christianity Today*:

> The writers of "The Mind Doctors" said of us that "Most of their critique centers on the fringes of psychology—with the fringes thus representing all psychology." Besides the therapies they list, we critique the following in our book *Psychological Way/The Spiritual Way*: psychoanalysts (Freud); client-centered therapy (Rogers); reality therapy (Glasser); and transactional analysis (Harris). According to a survey we did in cooperation with the Christian Association for Psychological Studies, these have been the most influential therapies in the practices of Christian therapists. Our books, including our recent *Psychoheresy*, are criticisms of mainline, not fringe, psychotherapy on the basis that it is not science, is not proven to be effective, and is known to harm. The use of psychotherapy and the

underlying psychologies in the church is not justified from either a scientific or biblical point of view. When used, it is always a slam at the sufficiency of the Word of God. Their response is correct in a sense. They do attack mainstream psychotherapies in their book. But their examples often come from extreme examples of bizarre therapies rather than the mainstream therapies. We randomly picked three psychotherapy textbooks from our shelves. None had a single paragraph devoted to scream therapy, encounter groups, est, arica, or transcendental meditation, yet a major portion of the Bobgans' book is devoted to these fringe therapies.

Other students of psychology have had similar experiences and feel the objections to psychology are often exaggerated. One letter we received from a graduate student in England read:

> I have been a Christian for eight years but until now have not had to work through anything very difficult. I have had quite negative responses from fellow Christians who are both ignorant about and afraid of psychology, and I feel rather at a loss over some of the issues.

Critics of psychology also tend to focus on relaxation and mental imagery, techniques used in some psychotherapies. Hunt and McMahon argue that since Eastern religions use imagery and positive thinking, all forms of these psychological tools are sorcery. Their arguments deserve to be considered carefully by Christian consumers of psychological services. However, an analysis of Hunt and McMahon's logic is also appropriate. They argue by association, concluding since A corresponds with B, and A is evil, then B is evil. Applying this line of thinking to other events shows some weakness in its logical structure. Since murderers drive cars and murder is evil, cars are evil. Since atheists read classical literature and atheism is evil, classical literature is evil. Since thieves wear gloves and stealing is wrong, gloves are wrong. Corresponding with A does not automatically make B evil. However, neither does it mean that B is not evil.

Arguing by association is falling prey to the correlation error. Of course it is exaggeration, but reasoning by association has been used to explain why fire engines are red: Fire

107

engines have eight firefighters and four wheels, eight and four is twelve, twelve inches is a foot, a foot is a ruler, Queen Elizabeth was a ruler, Queen Elizabeth was a ship, ships sail the seas, seas have fish, fish have fins, the Fins fought the Russians, Russians are red, so fire engines are red. Imagery and positive thinking techniques need to be carefully evaluated independent of their association with Eastern religions.

Asking the broad question, "Are psychotherapies spiritually dangerous?" will be of little value to Sharon since it fails to distinguish among the therapies. A more productive approach is to determine which psychotherapies are spiritually compatible with her beliefs and to discuss these perceptions with her pastor and her psychologist. After getting the pastor's and psychologist's perspectives on the technique to be used, additional information can be obtained by visiting the local library or perusing a general psychology textbook. Psychologists are bound by professional ethics to respect clients' wishes in terminating undesired techniques.

Is Psychotherapy Effective? ─────────────────────

For many years, psychologists believed that the personal values of a professionally trained psychologist would not affect psychotherapy. We now realize this is unrealistic; the personal values of therapists may indeed have an effect on the outcome of some treatments. Sometimes we hear of unscrupulous therapists who advise clients to have an affair to spice up their lives. From these appalling anecdotes, some resort to hasty generalization and assume all psychology is ineffective or immoral.

Kilpatrick and the Bobgans have questioned the effectiveness of psychotherapy and both cite a fascinating study of the outcome of psychotherapy conducted and reported by Hans Eysenck in 1952. Eysenck found those receiving psychotherapy had improved less after the treatment period than a group of subjects receiving no psychotherapy. It is not surprising that Eysenck's study caused a commotion in psychology.

Kilpatrick and the Bobgans fail, however, to also report that Eysenck's data have subsequently been analyzed by psychologist Allen Bergin. Bergin reported that Eysenck's analysis was contaminated by using different standards of improvement for the two groups of subjects. Also, Bergin objected to counting those who dropped out of treatment as treatment failures. From the same data that Eysenck concluded 39 percent improved with therapy, Bergin found 91 percent improved with therapy. It is a stunning discrepancy showing how both the practice and reporting of research can be guided by personal values and prior beliefs. Thirty-four years after the publication of Eysenck's report, we still conclude psychotherapy is not as effective as we would like, but numerous subsequent studies have been more hopeful. A 1980 review of 475 research studies on the results of psychotherapy suggests that psychotherapy is at least modestly effective.

Practicing psychologist Bernie Zilbergeld has correctly noted that counseling is not equally effective for all problems. But after the first few sessions, most experienced therapists will have a good estimate of potential treatment success. Of course, these estimates are hunches and cannot be considered completely accurate. In Sharon's case the possibilities are varied. If this is her first serious depression and if there are no physiological causes, she would be expected to improve rapidly with some forms of cognitive therapy. A recent study showed that fifteen of nineteen depressed clients recovered completely within twelve weeks after beginning cognitive psychotherapy. If, however, Sharon has been seriously depressed before or if there appears to be physiological imbalances, treatment might involve medication in conjunction with psychotherapy and could be prolonged.

As research has accumulated, it has become clear that there is little value in asking if psychotherapy works. Using the previous illustration, this is much like asking if toothpaste works. It depends on the brand and how it is applied. The more relevant question should be, "Is there a particular psychotherapy that will be effective for this client with this therapist?"

109

Can Psychology Tell Us Anything the Bible Can't? _____

In an article on Christian psychology, Jimmy Swaggart argues that the Bible is the only casebook for the cure of souls, and that psychology has its roots in atheism, evolution, and humanism.[4] Most Christian critics of psychology, like

Swaggart, take the position that theology is to be given authority over psychology, that psychology must be filtered through Scripture, and information inconsistent with Scripture must be rejected. Although there is an appealing simplicity in this approach, there are also several problems that limit its usefulness.

First, using the Bible to filter an academic discipline presumes that the Bible has something to say about all the questions asked in that particular discipline. This was the assumption that caused the church to discredit Galileo's belief in a sun-centered solar system, ranking special revelation above general revelation. As discussed in Chapter 2, all truth is God's truth but not all truth is in the Bible. There are ways of learning about God and His creation in addition to studying Scripture.

Few Christians would apply a scriptural filter to chemists, physicists, physiologists, or astronomers. Some justify this special treatment of psychology by stating that there are numerous inconsistencies between psychology and Christianity. But spending a few minutes leafing through a general psychology text will quickly dispel this idea. Conflicts with Scripture do not occur when discussing neuron function, brain hemisphere differences, sensory processes, psychophysics, perceptual development, memory systems, language development, problem solving, creativity, classical conditioning, and so on. The existing conflicts are limited to a narrow range of issues.

110   Second, Christians who want to check psychological findings against Scripture are creating a one-way street that is not healthy for either discipline. Giving theology authority over psychology, or any other science, prevents reciprocal feedback and integration that may benefit both disciplines. Using Scripture to filter astronomy led the church in 1615 to reject the unorthodox theory that the earth revolves around the sun and endorse the supposed scriptural position of an earth-centered universe.

In like manner, some critics argue for theological orthodoxy and dogma in opposition to psychological concepts. Kilpatrick and philosopher Robert Roberts authored *Christianity Today* articles examining the psychology of Carl

Rogers. Kilpatrick refers to Rogers' ideas as "radical," asserting that they ". . . run strongly counter to the orthodoxies and dogmas of the major Western religions." Likewise, Roberts writes, "Rogers is an optimist about human nature but a pessimist about culture, systems of morality, dogmas, and traditions. In this he is just the opposite of Christians . . . ."[5] Can we really equate Christianity with traditions, orthodoxies, and dogmas? Remember, the message of Christ was rejected by many because it wasn't orthodox. Consistency with established belief does not necessarily make something true. Automatically rejecting psychological concepts because they fail to fit existing church theologies is dangerous. Psychological concepts that oppose Christian tradition and dogma can be useful if they cause us to examine our faith more closely.

Finally, many Christians fail to integrate theology and psychology simply because they do not accept psychology as a science. Many critics of psychology continue to treat psychology as theology or philosophy. In the domain of science, theories come, compete with each other, are empirically tested, and go as the field edges toward truth. Psychology is best viewed as a set of proposed theories rather than a set of established facts. When it touches on truth, it touches on God's truth, because all truth is God's truth.

In dealing with Sharon's depression, the techniques used by a Christian psychologist may or may not involve the application of Scripture. But the methods used may reflect God's truth as discovered by human science.

A Valuable Controversy _____ 111

One goal of Christian life is to know God and His creation better, and the debate about the place of psychology in Christianity can cause us to better understand God's creation of human emotion and how He intended us to help those in need. Unfortunately, the Christian in need of psychological help often hears only one side of the debate. Thinking Christians need to carefully evaluate evidence on *both* sides of the debate in order to make informed decisions. It would be inappropriate for us to dogmatically defend all psychology because our critics have raised some valid concerns about modern psychology. Equally inappropriate is the rejection of all psychology because of incompatibilities between Christianity and a small part of the discipline. Only an openness on both sides and a frank exchange over all the issues will ultimately lead to a refined integration we can call Christian psychology.

There are some dangers intrinsic to psychological methods and practices, and Sharon would do well to maintain a healthy skepticism if she decides to seek psychotherapy. She might explore the psychologist's credentials, values, and treatment preferences prior to beginning any kind of therapy. Such an exploration is neither impolite nor unexpected. Critical thinkers ask questions.

If Sharon decides to seek professional counseling, there is potential for her to learn to view herself and her situation more accurately and, as a result, alleviate her depression. She might also be challenged in her faith as she confronts the dangers our critics have identified. Such challenges are part of natural Christian growth. In either case, under the care of a competent Christian psychologist, Sharon can benefit from the process, grow emotionally, and move ahead in her spiritual pilgrimage.

CHAPTER EIGHT

Humanism and The Christian

Four-year-old Kristin L. was found sitting in a pool of urine in the back seat of a 1975 Cadillac. Afraid her daughter would run away while she went to a nearby service station, her mother tied Kristin's wrists and ankles with electrical cords and fastened the cords to opposite sides of the car. In the midst of a 100° California day, with only one window slightly open, Kristin was left to baste in self-doubt and confusion. When the police finally came and rescued her, Kristin sobbed, "My mommy doesn't love me. Do you want to take me home?"

Kristin is probably an adolescent by now. But unless there has been miraculous intervention in her life, she is still struggling with self-worth. Because her mother rejected her, her teenage subconscious reasons that she deserves rejection and is worthless. Drugs, promiscuity, and parental defiance all could become ways for Kristin to seek an identity, to affirm her worth. But these efforts are futile and usually only lead to greater feelings of inadequacy and failure.

We cringe in pain when we hear about situations like Kristin's. We wonder how a mother could be so insensitive to the dignity of her child. Most all agree, regardless of religious or ideological persuasion, that Kristin's case is tragic. Kristin's worth was denied by the actions of her mother, and yet she does have worth. But why does Kristin have worth? Is it because she could someday become a Christian, or does she have worth simply because she is human?

The question of whether or not humans have intrinsic worth is yet another battle in the crossfire of ideas. Some conclude that just being human gives us worth that is unqualified and unequaled. Perhaps most of us feel that way when we hear of vivid cases like Kristin's (remember the vividness

113

effect). Others, though, insist that worth is only through redemption in Christ. They maintain that humans are fallen, depraved, and worthless, and that we can obtain worth only through a relationship with Jesus Christ.

What is the worth of a human being? Biologists inform us that the human body, if reduced to its chemical form, is worth very little. Isn't it ironic that we insure a body worth $1.50 (or is it $2.50 with inflation?) for $100,000 in case of death? If a family member has cancer, we gladly spend whatever is necessary for proper treatment. Lifetime savings are often spent in the last few weeks of a fleeting life. From one perspective, a person seems almost worthless. From another, we cherish humanity as priceless.

You're Worth It, or Are You? ⎯⎯⎯⎯⎯⎯⎯⎯⎯⎯⎯⎯

Advertisers tell us, "It costs a little more, but you're worth it!" This slogan affirms human worth. The human worth movement — humanism — has been influential in our culture. Humanistic values have affected our media, schools, public policy, and religious perspectives. As we have seen, this influence has created concern among many Christians including Tim LaHaye, the Gablers, Hunt and McMahon, and others.

A central theme of humanism is the dignity and worth of humans. Humanistic psychologist Carl Rogers has argued that human motivations and tendencies are intrinsically good. Furthermore, Rogers adds a dynamic component by suggesting individuals will spontaneously get better and better if obstacles are removed. Erich Fromm wrote that humans are fundamentally and basically good. Failing to attain one's full potential would be a personal tragedy, according to Fromm. Although more skeptical about the goodness of human nature, Abraham Maslow saw the mature person as one who recognizes the importance and worth of others. Humanists emphasize worth.

In contrast to the humanistic theme of worth and dignity is the Christian doctrine of human depravity. Humans, in themselves, are completely unable to save themselves from the consequences of sin. And evil is part of our very nature. (See Genesis 6:5, 8:21) "There is no one righteous, not even one; there is no one who understands, no one who seeks God."

(Romans 3:10-11; See also Psalm 14, 51; Ephesians 2:1-3, Romans 7:5.) Jesus told a parable recorded in Luke 18 related to human worth. Two men went to church, one of them quite assured of his worth; the other was not. The first, a Pharisee, stood praying to God with a self-righteous attitude: "God, thank you that I am better than others. Thank you that I don't cheat on my wife or in my business dealings. Thank you for making me such a wonderful person." The other, a tax-gatherer, couldn't even lift his eyes upward because of his humility. He beat his chest and said, "God, I am a sinner. Please have mercy." Jesus concluded, "For everyone who exalts himself will be humbled, and he who humbles himself will be exalted." The Scriptures are clear in their teaching that all descendants of Adam and Eve carry in their hearts the inheritance of sin (1 Corinthians 15:20-28). When we see ourselves as we are in God's sight, we should submit our hearts to Him in conformity to His will for a new life that He provides.

The Battle over Humanism

Human worth is central to humanism. Humanists believe that their hope for a wonderful future lies within the powers of humankind. Human depravity is fundamental in Christian theology, and both the Old and New Testaments teach that although humans are made in the image of God, they are under the power of sin. The focus of hope for Christians lies with Jesus Christ redeeming humans and nature to a state of perfection. Because humanists sometimes reject the God of the Bible as the source of values and the answer to humanity's deepest need, it is no wonder that humanists and Christians seem to be archenemies. Christians accuse humanists of conspiring to sway society to the "religion" of secular humanism. Humanists accuse Christians of absolute mindlessness. The battle escalates with new books and articles each year. Frequently, those in the debate that are the loudest have an incomplete understanding of the other side — a breach of intellectual etiquette. Thinking critically about humanism is a valuable skill for Christians living on the battlefield of ideas.

Because humanists and Christians don't always think critically, there has been distortion from both groups. A well-known Christian speaker once observed that abortion is taught as an alternative to birth control and that we could expect more of the same as long as society was led by a secular humanistic worldview. He went on to say that secular humanism denies the worth of humans. Although many humanists advocate abortion, this speaker was incorrect in saying humanists don't care about the worth of humans. This is a distortion of the humanistic position since the worth of individuals is the very basis of humanism.

Humanists are also guilty of distorting the Christian perspective. One humanist referred to Christians as "the crazies." Humanists often identify Christians as those fanatics who bomb abortion clinics. Most Christians are not crazy. Most humanists are not crazy. Christians identify humanists as something they are not and humanists do the same to Christians. The resulting crossfire of emotionally charged salvos is fierce and largely unnecessary because it has grown out of ignorance. In most cases, neither side fully understands the other's position. This emotional reaction makes it difficult to discern the real differences between humanism and Christianity.

Broadly-defined Systems

Christianity and humanism are based on many different assumptions and neither can be easily summarized. Christianity is based on the teachings of Jesus Christ and the practice of what He commanded. As such, it promotes a specific view of God, humans, sin, creation, and atonement, and advocates practices that are ethical, ritualistic, and devotional. But as the presence of hundreds of diverse Christian denominations indicates, the expression of Christian beliefs takes many forms.

Humanism also exists in many forms. We hear about humanism in public education, secular humanism, Christian humanism, psychological humanism, and so on. In his book, *Is Man the Measure?*, Dallas Theological Seminary professor Norman Geisler describes many different forms of humanism including evolutionary humanism, behavioral humanism, existential humanism, pragmatic humanism, Marxist humanism, egocentric humanism, cultural humanism, and Christian humanism. All these forms of humanism have slightly different emphases. Some forms of humanism are secular in that they do not include a concept of God. Evolutionary humanists deny the existence of God by suggesting God is only an idea that humans have created as a psychological entity. Others, pragmatic humanists, have avoided religious explanations in preference to natural explanations for the events of the world. Many of the assumptions of natural science, politics, and education can be traced to the pragmatic humanism of John Dewey and others.

Geisler also describes Christian humanism. Christian author C. S. Lewis's writings form a sort of Christian humanism in that they affirm the dignity, creativity, and moral integrity of humankind. When we teach our children that God cared enough for them to send His only Son, we are teaching them a form of Christian humanism. Christ dignified the human condition with His sacrificial death.

So humanism, like Christianity, is a diverse set of beliefs that takes on many different forms. In recognition of its diverse nature, humanism can be defined as a set of philosophies endorsing the dignity and worth of human beings.

Figure 1 illustrates the relationship between humanism and Christianity. Humanism and Christianity are separate philosophical systems (areas A and C), but some tenets are shared between the two (area B). It is easy to focus only on the

HUMANISM AND CHRISTIANITY

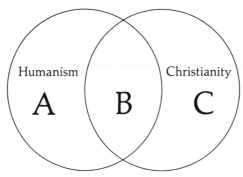

117

A and C are areas of incompatibility between humanism and Christianity. B is the area of compatibility between the two.

Figure 1

differences between the two belief systems as many Christian and humanist authors have done. Unfortunately, the result of such a focus can be a crossfire that creates confusion. But remember our definition of humanism. Is it incompatible to believe both in the dignity and worth of humans and the deity and atoning work of Jesus Christ?

Of course, some forms of humanism are incompatible with Christianity. These humanisms are found in area A of Figure 1.

Some forms of humanism have obvious dangers. In 1933, thirty-four American humanists, including educator John Dewey, philosopher Edwin Burtt, and Unitarian minister R. Lester Mondale, endorsed a philosophy of religious humanism called the *Humanist Manifesto*. The manifesto advocated evolutionary, naturalistic, and atheistic explanations for the universe. The document was updated in the 1973 *Humanist Manifesto II* in which the humanist mandates were stated more strongly than in the 1933 version. But characterizing all humanists by the humanist manifestos is no more accurate than characterizing all Christians by a single denominational worldview.

Christian Roots

Many cringe at the mere suggestion that humanists have found some truth. Perhaps this is because we have learned in recent years to think of humanism as evil and seductive. Dr. Nelson Bell, quoted in *Secular Humanism: The Most Dangerous Religion in America*, states:

118

> Today, within the bounds of the Church, we are witnessing a satanic work of deception and substitution that is intended to deceive even the very elect. This giant hoax is the *substitution of humanism for Christianity* (italics not added).[1]

Such a view is simplistic and overlooks important facts about humanism and its development.

Humanism and Protestantism both have roots in the Renaissance and have some similar emphases. Both emphasize freedom, responsibility, and concern for others. Yet current opponents of humanism look at a small part of the Renaissance and use it to conclude that humanism has always been evil. Tim LaHaye writes:

> The giant replica of Michelangelo's magnificent David stands nude, overlooking the beautiful city. Quite naturally, this contradicts the wisdom of God, for early in Genesis, the Creator followed man's folly by giving him animal skins to cover his nakedness. Ever since, there has been a conflict concerning clothes, with man demanding the freedom to go naked. The Renaissance obsession with nude "art forms" was the forerunner of the modern humanist's demand for pornography in the name of freedom.[2]

Making a Straw Man

Tim LaHaye's position on Renaissance humanism deserves a reader's skepticism. First, he implicitly assumes humanists advocate pornography. Later in his book, he writes:

> ... these educators inundate the minds of our youth with humanistic theology from kindergarten through college, teaching them that marijuana is not harmful (scientific evidence and reports notwithstanding); encouraging the use of drugs; advocating the freedom to use pornographic magazines (and, in some cases, assigning pornographic literature in the place of the classics); ridiculing the values of their parents and free-enterprise system; downgrading patriotism, and creating an obsession with everything but a quality education.[3]

One component of critical thinking is comparing extreme claims with life experience. In a recent Oregon election, a bill legalizing the possession of marijuana was defeated by a landslide. If, as LaHaye asserts, humanists who believe in drugs and pornography are taking over society, infiltrating our schools, and dominating the television airwaves, why would such a bill be so soundly defeated in the most unchurched state in the Union? Most humanists do not believe in the things LaHaye describes. He would be hard pressed to find even an extremist who would adopt all of these positions! Humanists do not support pornography; many are concerned about the exploitation of women and children and are involved in the fight against pornography.

LaHaye's reference to Renaissance art as pornographic is equally questionable. The dictionary defines pornography as obscene art or literature. To equate Renaissance art and literature with obscenity is unreasonable because Renaissance art reflects an era of intellectual freedom where any image, including the human body, could be the subject of artistic inquiry. This is very different from modern pornography, which focuses on sexual license and irresponsibility. LaHaye would have us return to the classics, but even "classics" involve concepts or ideas that are threatening to some Christians. The diversity of thinking or reasoning by Christians would make selecting a "safe" set of works virtually impossible. God provided animal skins for Adam and Eve because they were ashamed, not because nudity was intrinsically evil. Today nudity is often a stimulus for evil, especially in pornography. But even this varies from culture to culture with what would be considered sexually stimulating in one culture eliciting no response in another culture. Today's sinful tendencies do not justify the conclusion that Michelangelo's masterpiece was pornographic.

Finally, even if we agree that Michelangelo sculpted pornography, LaHaye selects a small portion of the Renaissance to illustrate the evil influence of humanism. By selecting a small part of the Renaissance, his persuasion may be effective, but it does not represent the Renaissance as a whole. The Renaissance was a tremendous time of "rebirth" and enlightenment. Enormous progress occurred in promoting free thought and inquiry, including freedom to develop the physical and social sciences. Christianity was revolutionized with the Reformation. These positive changes could be equated with humanism as easily as Michelango's art.

Christian critics of humanism have created a "straw man." By making humanism seem worse than it really is, they can convince themselves and others of its threat to Christianity. But straw men don't do any real damage. And if we spend all our time battling straw men, the actual weaknesses of humanistic thought can sneak by us.

A publication by the Institute of Basic Youth Conflicts also creates a humanistic straw man. The Jonestown tragedy is presented as "the ultimate illustration of humanism." Ironically, atheistic humanists use this very instance to demonstrate the failures of organized religion. The humanists don't want

Jim Jones any more than the Christians. To illustrate the failure of humanism with the Jonestown tragedy distracts us from the real weaknesses of humanism.

Some secular forms of humanism are based on atheistic assumptions and many Christians have responded firmly and properly by opposing these forms of humanism. But others have gone too far in sounding the alarm. As the battle escalates, we run the risk of forgetting the humanistic truths promoted by our Christian forerunners. We even run the risk of ignoring truth found in Scripture that is consistent with humanistic thought. In our zeal to purge the church of humanism, we might easily discard biblical truth as well. If we removed all of humanism from Figure 1, we would end up losing part of Christianity as shown in Figure 2.

CHRISTIANITY WITHOUT HUMANISM

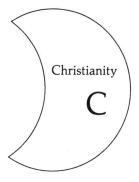

If all humanistic influences are removed, Christianity is left without some of its most powerful doctrine.

Figure 2

Areas of Compatibility

Taking such a bite out of Christianity would be unfortunate because humanism and Christianity share some important elements that seem to be unnoticed in the crossfire. Consider four similarities between Christianity and humanism.

First, both Christians and humanists focus on human experience. Christians believe in the worth of humans, as created in God's image, and they emphasize social justice and compassion. Similarly, humanistic psychologists have rejected a mechanistic and deterministic view of humanity in favor of seeing humans as creative, transcendent, and controlled by personal values and choices. The American Association of Humanistic Psychology includes the following in its statement of aims: "A centering of attention on the experiencing person and thus a focus on experience as the primary phenomenon in the study of man."[4] This recognition of the uniqueness and importance of human experience echoes Christian theology.

Christians view Christ's death as a result of God's concern for the human condition. Indeed, humanity was honored by a sign of divine glory in the incarnation of Jesus Christ. In His sacrificial death He manifested the most positive of divine and human characteristics. Further, His death showed that He valued humanity highly enough to be exploited rather than exercising dominance over creation. Christians and humanists are similar in that they both place priority on humanity.

There is obvious danger in taking this too far. God is not a humanist. God is concerned for humanity but within the context of His character and grace. Parents can understand this concept out of their experience. Good parents are always concerned for their children, but they recognize that good parenting involves more than letting children do whatever they want to do. They actively exercise an appropriate amount of control over the actions and decisions of their children, hoping their children will, in time, develop a fuller awareness of reality. The child allowed complete freedom is hopelessly lost without structure or direction. Parents believe in children, but they are concerned about more than just childhood. Likewise, God believes in us, but is concerned with more than just humanity. He sees the bigger picture and works in our lives so that we can see more of His view as we grow spiritually.

A second similarity between humanism and Christianity is that both advocate personal responsibility. The Christians creating humanistic straw men would have us think otherwise, but humanists have been very concerned about responsibility. A mark of personal maturity, according to humanistic psychologist Gordon Allport, is the ability to set and strive for goals. Abraham Maslow wrote, "Human beings seem to be far more autonomous and self-governed than modern psychology

122

theory makes allowance for."[5] Carl Rogers described the mature person as one who can cope with the stress of life while maintaining self-direction and a true acceptance of others.

Christians also believe in personal responsibility. If we want to change something about ourselves, we seek God's help and go about making the appropriate changes. If we sense a need for greater evangelism, we set up programs and try to reach those in need. If our churches and institutions need more money, we seek to raise funds. If we have a problem, we seek responsible solutions.

At first this may seem like an obvious similarity. Doesn't everyone believe in responsibility? But personal responsibility implies personal freedom and freedom is not a component of all philosophies. Both behaviorism and Freudian psychoanalysis are deterministic. That is, they deny personal freedom. According to these philosophical systems, our current behavior depends completely on our past experiences and our biological makeup. Determinists say we may believe we have freedom, but it is only a delusion. Humanism and Christianity stand in opposition to radical determinism. Both believe in personal responsibility and freedom.

Third, both Christianity and humanism emphasize human worth. At the very heart of humanism is its emphasis on the dignity and worth of human beings. Remember four-year-old Kristin? She sobbed to a policeman, "Do you want to take me home?" and "My mommy doesn't love me." Probably the responses of a humanist and a Christian would be very similar. Both would feel a heartrending compassion for an abused little girl. Both would seek ways of helping Kristin. Both would perceive the tragedy of a child without a sense of worth. In the words of R. B. Cunningham, "Christians agree with humanists that human beings have an inviolable dignity and worth and are the central value within the natural process."[6]

In recent years, Christians have started talking and writing more about self-worth. We now hear not only about our depravity but also about being made in God's image. Both worth and depravity are biblical concepts (see Genesis 1:27, 5:1-2; Jeremiah 17:9; Matthew 15:17-20; Romans 3:10-23; 1 Corinthians 11:7; Ephesians 2:1-3; James 3:9; 1 Peter 3:4),

123

but until recently depravity was emphasized much more than worth. In the last decade many books have appeared about loving ourselves. These are healthy additions to our traditional emphases of sin and inadequacy, but from where did they come? It is probably not a coincidence that the humanism of the sixties and seventies has evoked a greater awareness of human worth within the church. Humanism has not changed our doctrine, but it has influenced which parts of our doctrine are emphasized. Ironically, at the same time Christian extremists are attacking humanism, the rest of us are embracing humanistic values by focusing more on doctrines of worth.

Finally, both humanists and Christians are concerned for social justice and the rights of the oppressed. "Humanists . . . are passionately humanitarian in their concern for the good life and for social justice."[7] Similarly, the teachings of Jesus were frequently related and directed to those with hardships and misfortunes, and social interest was a function of one's involvement in the body of Christ (see Matthew 25:35-40). Jesus spoke of comfort for the poor, the hungry, and those who mourn (Matthew 5:3-12). An emphasis on justice and human rights is essential to the credibility of the church.

Areas of Incompatibility

Although there are more areas of compatibility than extremists acknowledge, we must be careful not to assume humanism and Christianity are the same. Critics of humanism have legitimate concerns, and there are distinct incompatibilities between the two philosophical systems.

124

For some, belief in human potential has replaced a belief in God. These humanists are antisupernatural. That is, they believe either that God does not exist or that He is not an important influence in our world. This hidden assumption can be subtle and sneak up on Christians. Sometimes we begin to place too much confidence in ourselves, forgetting we serve an all-powerful God.

A second area of incompatibility has to do with Christian calling. As mentioned earlier, both Christians and humanists believe in personal responsibility, but some humanists take this farther than Christians. Personal responsibility is the ultimate reality for some humanists. For those with antisupernatural assumptions there is no higher power to direct their paths, so they accept complete responsibility for their destiny. In contrast, Christians believe in divine intervention. We believe in responsibility, but we constantly recognize God's power to open and close options in our lives. The extreme humanist sees no greater power than humanity.

Third, Christians have a balanced view of human worth. Humanists believe in human worth, but often fail to balance worth with potential for evil. Carl Rogers believed that we are all born with an actualizing tendency, the natural inclination to get better and better. Christians, however, balance their belief in human worth with a realistic perspective of the potential for evil. When a teased six-year-old comes home from school, eyes cast downward and head bowed, the child illustrates the human tendency for evil. Why are the other kids so cruel? Life experience tells us that human worth is balanced with potential for evil. Humanistic perspectives denying this side of humankind are incomplete.

Even secular psychologists have criticized humanistic assumptions of total human goodness as unrealistic and naive. Humanism has established itself as a permanent force in psychology, but because of its overly optimistic perspective of human nature, it never came to dominate psychology as its founders expected.

So humanism and Christianity have areas of compatibility and incompatibility. Critical thinkers can look at both humanistic and Christian thought in their search for God's truth. But in the search for truth, we need to be cautious of false alarms. Like the "boy who cried wolf," Christians may be losing credibility by sounding unnecessary alarms. After enough false alarms, people may stop listening and dismiss all concerns about humanism, even valid concerns, as propaganda. But Christians are not the only ones sounding false alarms. Humanists are fighting back with their own extremist positions.

False Alarms from Both Extremes _____

1. *Self-esteem is harmful to your spiritual health.* Some have argued that humanism, with its emphasis on self-esteem and

self-worth, is a bad influence on society. Hunt and McMahon write:

> The Scriptures differ with the current assessment that many of mankind's problems arise from a deficiency of self-esteem or self-love. In contrast, the apostle Paul warns that self-love in the end times will be at the root of such problems. Are we seeing this prophecy fulfilled in our day?[8]

They go on to suggest our only value comes through redemption in Christ.

But other Christians have different perspectives. In a church bulletin insert, Alvin Price was quoted as saying, "Parents need to fill a child's bucket of self-esteem so high that the rest of the world can't poke enough holes in it to drain it dry." Who is right? Should we build self-esteem or deny it?

As psychologists, we have seen many who do not accept God's love, not because they have inadequate spiritual training, but because they believe themselves to be unlovable. Once they can accept themselves, they can reach out in faith to God more completely. Self-image and self-love are not synonyms.

2. *Humanism is a well-organized conspiracy.* A common assertion is that humanism is a conspiracy to subvert Christian thought. Some Christian authors suggest humanists exist in strategic places in the government and in broadcasting companies in order to influence society. In some ways, they are correct. Undoubtedly, extremist humanists exist at every level of public and private enterprise. They seek to evangelize others and persuade them of the merits of humanism. But we need to be careful not to introduce a double standard. We advocate Christian evangelism, but become upset when a competing philosophy attempts to evangelize. We call their efforts a conspiracy and our efforts genuine concern for others.

The presence of this double standard is clear in one author's comparison of humanism and communism. According to the author, both seek to control the educational system, both seek to destroy all religions except their own, both seek the betterment of the human race, and both seek the allegiance of wayward Christians.[9] There are two problems with this analysis. First, the author has succumbed to the correlation error and is arguing by association. Second, the same list of commonalities could apply to Christianity and communism. We could even add others. For example, the early church had a history of communal living. The fact that humanism and communism share some common assumptions does not imply they are coconspiracies.

3. *Christianity denies human freedom.* A quick look through a magazine like *The Humanist* makes it clear that Christians are not the only ones sounding false alarms. Some extreme humanists are fighting just as hard as Christian extremists and are outspoken in their condemnation of God-centered religions. As we have seen, Christian concerns range from legitimate to absurd. As might be expected, humanist criticisms of Christianity cover a similar range.

One common humanist complaint is that Christianity denies human freedom. Because we believe in obedience to a higher power, they assume we are less free. In some ways they are correct. We are less free to determine our destiny because we believe in divine guidance. In other ways, though, they have misunderstood Christianity. Psychologist George Albee has written this about Christianity: "... one was saved if one was rigidly moral and successful in one's calling, and one was damned if one was an economic or moral failure."[10] What a distortion of the tenets of Christianity! We are saved by the grace of God and not by our own works (Ephesians 2:8-9). Similarly, Erich Fromm suggested the goals of religion to be obedience and powerlessness, resulting in a prevailing mood of sorrow. Christianity results in just the opposite: power for goodness and peace and joy.

127

4. *Christianity rewards passivity.* A second humanistic criticism is that Christianity rewards passivity. Humanists see Christians as those who sit in rocking chairs waiting for divine instruction about whether to have grilled cheese or a BLT for lunch. Again, this is largely unfounded. Some Christians seem to be hopelessly reflective and indecisive, but not most. Christianity is a call to action, not a call to passivity. Social relief organizations, rescue missions, homeless shelters, foreign missionary hospitals and clinics, and political activism are all examples of Christian activities that have made a difference in our world.

5. *Christians use guerrilla tactics.* Another common humanistic criticism is that Christianity uses guerrilla tactics. These unethical tactics are allegedly necessary because of the weakness of the Christian position. In making this assertion, humanists fall prey to hasty generalization. Most Christians do not bomb abortion clinics. The extreme humanistic world-view condemns all Christians as co-conspirators, just as Christians often view all humanists as part of a large conspiracy.

Although it is an overgeneralization, it appears to be true that some Christians use guerrilla tactics. For example, Christians are generally opposed to situational ethics, and yet some practice a situational ethic in responding to humanists. One Christian author writes, "[The humanist] lives like a leech, drawing a fat salary off of the system that he seeks to destroy."[11] Even if this accusation were true, and it isn't, would it justify such statements? Since the Christian cause is perceived as so important, any means of battle becomes justifiable. After all, we are battling for eternal souls. Unfortunately, the importance of the cause combined with the stress of the crossfire can lead even Christians to situationally justify slander, misrepresentation, and even bombing.

In the crossfire of false alarms and valid warnings about humanism, Christians must think critically and look for truth wherever it can be found. As we consider sending our hard-earned money for hunger relief in third-world countries, we need to remember the humanistic emphasis on human dignity and worth. As we struggle with temptation, we need to remember the humanistic emphasis on free choice and responsibility. But in deciding where to send our money, we also need to remember the Christian message of human depravity and the need for Christ's love. So we find an organization that feeds hungry people with food and Christian truths. And in dealing with temptation, we need to remember that human freedom does not supersede God's commandments for moral living. So we seek to obey God as we freely choose our actions. Christians who think critically can find truth in humanism while holding firm to the essentials of Christian thought.

128

CHAPTER NINE

What About Public Education?

David and Cheryl have been reading articles as they consider whether to send their child to public or private school. Some authors argue that public schools are filled with secular humanists who teach children evil philosophies. Other authors insist Christian schools are rigid and narrow. David and Cheryl are new Christians who want the best possible education for their child. They find the crossfire of conflicting messages to be confusing.

David and Cheryl are facing another issue on the battlefield of ideas. They want to make a good decision about their children's education, weighing the facts carefully and considering both sides. They want to be critical thinkers who don't fall prey to freezethink in the midst of such a crucial decision. What they read is confusing and frightening.

The Good Old Days ———————————————————

Many Christian parents are concerned about the deterioration of public schools. In *The Battle for the Mind*, Tim LaHaye asserts humanists have deliberately seized Western education in order to control the minds of humankind. One speaker at a 1986 conference sponsored by Christian Reconstructionists (those who believe Christians should work to establish a theocracy in our current political system), and covered by *Christianity Today*, stated that public schools are under Satan's control, suggesting public educators are deliberately reducing the reading and writing skills of American students in order to make them more vulnerable to socialism. Others at the conference made similar claims. A pastor and head of a private Christian school stated that Christian parents commit "blasphemy against Jesus Christ" when they allow their children to attend public schools.

Critical thinking involves questioning such extreme claims. By overstating and oversimplifying, some Christian critics have misrepresented past and present public education. According to a booklet published by the Institute of Basic Youth Conflicts, "Secular humanism is now the established religion in American public schools."[1] Humanistic education started, according to the booklet, when John Dewey signed the *Humanist Manifesto* in 1933, one year after serving as president of the National Education Association. This oversimplified history of education implies that all the humanistic influence can be traced back to a single person and a specific manifesto. But what about the following quote?

> The essence of education is that it be religious. . . . what is religious education? A religious education is an education which inculcates duty and reverence. Duty arises from our potential control over the course of events. Where attainable knowledge could have changed the issue, ignorance has the guilt of vice. And the foundation of reverence is this perception, that the present holds within itself the complete sum of existence, backwards and forwards, the whole amplitude of time, which is eternity. [2]

At first glance this quote, from a book entitled *The Aims of Education*, supports the notion that educators define religion in humanistic terms. The educator writing this quote suggests the chief aim of religion is to control the events of this world (humans as sovereign, rather than God) and that there is nothing more to this material cosmos than what is now (denial of the supernatural). It appears that Dewey's influence has been devastating. Right? Our schools used to be filled with godly instruction and now they're filled with the kind of humanism seen in the above quote. Right?

But this quote isn't from a modern-day humanist trying to control our schools. It was written before Dewey signed the *Humanist Manifesto* and before he was president of the National Education Association. Published in 1929, the quote comes from an education expert of the day, Alfred North Whitehead. So it seems inaccurate to view the current or past problems with public education to be the result of one man or one manifesto. Maybe the education issue isn't as clear-cut as some imply. Maybe humanism in education has been around

130

for a long time. Maybe the "good old days" when they taught Christianity in the public schools have been exaggerated a bit.

Believing the public schools are controlled by humanists trying to persuade our children to be atheistic evolutionists is appealing in its simplicity. Such a belief contributes to freezethink by giving us a simple way to think about the problems with public education. But sometimes simple ways of thinking are not accurate. Conversely, it is tempting to dismiss all critics of public education as paranoid. But even if Christian extremists have presented flawed arguments, parts of their arguments may be valid. A report developed by Connecticut Mutual Life suggests the values of educators are more liberal than the values of the public; fewer educators are opposed to abortion, divorce, or homosexuality; seventy-three percent of the general population believe God loves them, while forty percent of educators believe the same.[3] If that is the case, maybe some public education is a threat to our children.

Are the opponents of public education sounding an important alarm about the dangers of entrusting our children to public schools, or are they overreacting to trends in education that have been in America for decades already? Should Christian values be taught in public schools, in private schools, or at home? Is it always wrong to send our children to public schools? These questions are natural in response to varied opinions held by Christians about public education. How is the thinking Christian to respond? Two key questions are presented to stimulate critical thinking about public education: (1) Are public schools teaching humanism? and (2) Are schools effective?

131

Are Public Schools Teaching Humanism?

The answer to this question depends on one's definition of humanism. One Christian publication states, "Neutral education is . . . impossible. Teaching knowledge without God is the religion of humanism."[4] Using this definition, public education is humanism, but notice how the author forces ideas into one of two categories (dichotomous thinking). The author implies that if knowledge isn't specifically related to God (and, by implication, to Christian beliefs), then it is the religion of humanism. It assumes there are only two ways of thinking—Christianity and humanism.

Humanism or humanistic religion? Many Christian extremists refer to humanism as a religion, presumably because humanism opposes Christianity in some ways. Some humanists, like the signers of the humanist manifestos, described their beliefs as religious humanism. But not all humanists are religious humanists. It is an important distinction because words shape thought and thoughts shape our attitudes and observations. (Remember, we see what we believe, as discussed in Chapter 3.) If we believe humanism is a religion, then we view the actions of humanists as deliberate efforts to convert or deceive us. An alternative is to see humanism as a set of diverse philosophies, some compatible and some not compatible with Christianity. Tim LaHaye demonstrates the power of considering humanism a religion when he writes, "Humanism is not only the world's greatest evil but, until recently, the most deceptive of all religious philosophies."[5]

A similar confusion can be seen among those calling themselves Christians. When national polls indicate sixty percent of the American people consider themselves Christians, it does not mean sixty percent adhere to a committed evangelical Christian lifestyle or hold to an orthodox Christian faith. Rather, it reflects a heritage of Christian culture and a general set of beliefs about morality. Similarly, not all humanists are religious humanists. Some hold to the philosophical assumptions of humanism, such as the dignity and freedom of humans, while believing in God.

132

Specific religious doctrines cannot be authorized as the correct religion in public schools, but principles derived from humanism and Christianity can be taught. This distinction is shown in Table 1. Columns A and D represent a sampling of doctrines from atheistic humanism and Christianity, none of which can be formally endorsed in public schools. Neither Christianity nor religious humanism can be presented as the correct religion because of separation of church and state. This symmetry in what cannot be taught is often overlooked by critics of public education. The same Christian publication that asserts "every American public school is a school of Humanism" also cites the following Supreme Court decision:

> The State may not establish a "religion of secularism" in the sense of affirmatively opposing or showing hostility to religion, thus "preferring those who believe in no religion over those who do believe."[6]

Although doctrines cannot be presented as state religions, moral principles derived from those doctrines can be taught. Columns B and C show some principles drawn from humanism and Christianity that can be taught. As discussed in Chapter 8, some of the principles derived from Christianity and humanism are identical.

HUMANISM AND CHRISTIANITY IN PUBLIC EDUCATION

A	B	C	D
Doctrines of Atheistic Humanism	Moral Principles of Humanism	Moral Principles of Christianity	Doctrines of Christianity
Universe was not created	Scientific evolution	Scientific creationism	Created world There is one
No supernatural being	Personal freedom	Freedom/ accountability	God known only through
Highest goal is fulfillment of human life	Personal responsibility	Personal responsibility	Jesus Christ Highest goal is to love and
	Seek satisfying life	Seek pure life	serve God
	Dignity of human life	Dignity of human life	
	Moral living	Moral living	
	Self-esteem	Respecting authority	
	Serving others	Serving others	

Table 1

133

The content of public school classroom instruction also depends on the values of teachers, administrators, board members, and parents. Although some topics are prescribed by school curriculum policies, many topics are left to teachers' discretion. Some teachers will choose to teach scientific creationism while others will only teach evolutionary theory. Some will teach about death and dying and others will avoid these topics.

It is important to recognize the difference between humanism and religious humanism in order to avoid dichotomous thinking. Because Christian doctrines *are not* taught, some use dichotomous thinking to conclude that atheistic humanist doctrines *are* being taught. So we read statements such as ". . . educators inundate the minds of our youth with humanistic theology from kindergarten through college" and "Every American school is a school of Humanism."

The principles of humanism, with their focus on personal responsibility, often have positive influence in education. It is a humanistic principle when Sarah learns to do the very best she can in a first grade spelling test. Sarah learns she can improve her performance with sincere effort. She doesn't learn to pray for God's help before the spelling test, but neither is she learning a competitive religion. In fact, the message of personal effort is consistent with Christian beliefs. Paul frequently used athletic analogies to encourage his readers to put their best efforts into their faith. We are to "fight the good fight of the faith" (1 Timothy 6:12) and "run with perseverance the race marked out for us." (Hebrews 12:1) Teaching personal effort in public education can fit well with a child's faith in God.

If she is told, "Sarah, I want you to forget about your ideas of God and rely on your own abilities to take this test," then she is being taught the competitive religion of humanism. Christians should be concerned about education that overtly opposes reliance on God, but most teachers would not tell Sarah to forget about God.

134

Perhaps some do want to infuse humanistic religion in the schools just as some Christians want the Christian religion in the schools. Some are as persuaded of the merits of humanism as we are the merits of Christianity. Humanist Ronald Miller suggests "it is within our power . . . to give education an entirely new meaning — a humanistic one . . . if that is the kind of world we choose to inhabit."[7]

Some humanists want to promote their atheistic religion in public education. These are the humanists quoted by Christians who are concerned about humanism in the school. But individual quotes do not necessarily indicate a large-scale problem. Remember the vividness effect.

To develop an accurate understanding of the dangers and merits of humanism, we should also read the writings of those who employ humanistic principles without advocating a humanistic religion. In reading the goals for humanistic education published by the Association for Supervision and Curriculum Development in Washington, D.C., one finds that many of the goals of humanistic education are completely compatible with ideals Christian parents have for their children — responsibility, creativity, and independent thinking, for example.

As we've argued in previous chapters, an entire field cannot be evaluated by the fringes. Just because some advocates of religious humanism are outspoken, it does not necessarily follow that all educators are trying to lead our children into a competing faith. Education cannot be evaluated by the humanistic fringes any more than it can be evaluated by the Christian fringes. Yet some extremist writers perpetuate the humanism scare with statements such as "Humanism, as taught in public school textbooks, clearly fits the definition of a religion."[8] How can all textbooks be lumped together into a single category? This appeals to dichotomous thinkers, but has to be questioned by critical thinkers.

Finding truth in humanism. Because Christian extremists malign the intent of humanism, we sometimes develop inaccurate ideas about humanists. One Christian pamphlet reports that the ultimate act of humanism is suicide. Humanism, however, stands for human growth and potential, not human death! Suicide is abhorrent for humanists as it is for Christians. Similarly, extreme humanists malign Christians. It's too bad, because we could learn from each other. Humanists and Christians both value integrity, wisdom, and resourcefulness. Humanists don't promote drugs, spread AIDS, and spawn cults like some Christians suggest. They promote many wholesome qualities, some quite compatible with Christian thinking. Similarly, Christians aren't the "crazies" as atheistic humanists often suggest. The crossfire is fierce.

We studied the compatibility of humanism and Christianity by developing a questionnaire to measure attitudes about humanism.[9] The questionnaire had three parts:

humanism as defined by educators, humanism as defined by psychologists, and humanism as defined by opposing Christian writers. We gave the questionnaire to Christian college and community college students to validate the scale. After demonstrating its validity, we gave the questionnaire to another sample of Christian college students along with other questionnaires, including one measuring Christian commitment. Not surprisingly, those endorsing the atheistic humanism to which Christian writers object were less committed in their Christian faith.

In contrast, agreement with the humanistic principles defined by educators was positively related to Christian beliefs. Highly committed Christians actually endorsed humanistic principles more than less committed Christians.

In their zeal, some Christian authors have overstated the incompatibility of humanism and Christianity. Most Christians object to the extreme form of humanism they describe, but they are not describing mainstream humanism. Mainstream humanism was quite agreeable to Christians in our study, especially the committed Christians.

Because of the subtle influences of groupthink, Christians sometimes close their minds prematurely to the value of humanism in education. It was interesting to watch two philosophers, one a Christian and the other a humanist, discuss public education on *The John Ankerberg Show*. John Ankerberg, an evangelical and the host of the television program, invites people representative of cults and non-Christian religions and philosophies to a half-hour, unrehearsed debate of their beliefs with a Christian guest. Throughout the debate, the Christian was rude, disparaging, and unreasonable in his attacks. The patience of the humanist was a better example of godly behavior than the abuse given by the Christian. The man arguing the humanist position was trying to make the point that public schools can teach religion but they cannot hold to an authorized state religion. But he hardly had a chance to explain his points because the Christian kept interrupting with antihumanist propaganda, most of which was exaggerated and sensationalistic.

We don't have to agree with humanism. But if our Christian faith is as strong as we think, we should at least understand the real humanism of the public schools (as defined by humanists) before deciding to reject it. In the process of understanding humanism, most find there are some refreshing and helpful perspectives that are consistent with Christian faith.

Humanism and self-sufficiency. One problem with Western society is our emphasis on individualism and self-sufficiency. In their excellent book, *Habits of the Heart,* Robert Bellah and colleagues discuss the negative effects of a society obsessed with individualism. We have lost much of our vision of caring for a larger community and establishing our identity with a cohesive group. We so easily identify with the song lyrics, "I did it my way." When self-sufficiency goes too far there is no room for God.

Think about movie heroes. John Wayne, a prototype of twentieth century individualism, has been replaced with new heroes that defy the establishment, succeed at whatever they want, and promote personal independence. Indiana Jones, Rambo, and James Bond succeed on their own, in spite of impossible odds. Our heroes are self-sufficient. We sometimes even view heroes in the church as self-sufficient. Dr. X has published thirty-five books and is a widely sought lecturer. Pastor Y helped his church to grow from 25 to 250 in five years. Paul had the same temptation to be self-sufficient:

> If anyone else thinks he has reasons to put confidence in the flesh, I have more: circumcised on the eighth day, of the people of Israel, of the tribe of Benjamin, a Hebrew of Hebrews; in regard to the law, a Pharisee; as for zeal, persecuting the church; as for legalistic righteousness, faultless. But whatever was to my profit I now consider loss for the sake of Christ. What is more, I consider everything a loss compared to the surpassing greatness of knowing Christ Jesus my Lord, for whose sake I have lost all things. I consider them rubbish, that I may gain Christ . . . . (Philippians 3:4-8)

137

Because Paul had been a hero, a leader among religious leaders, he struggled with self-sufficiency. Elsewhere he described his boasting as foolish (2 Corinthians 11:16 – 12:1). Paul recognized his struggle and tried to affirm his dependence on God, even to the point of counting his accomplishments as rubbish.

Some believe humanism leads children down a path of excessive self-sufficiency, teaching them to look out for their own needs rather than considering the needs of their peers. This would be hard to prove or disprove, but humanists have historically been committed to building community relations and interdependence rather than isolated self-reliance. It may be humanism, our Judeo-Christian heritage, or some other factor that causes self-sufficiency. Whatever the cause, helping children balance a healthy sense of self-reliance with appreciation for God's provision and dependence on Him is a noble goal for parents.

The perfect balance for our children is to help them be self-confident while avoiding self-sufficient pride. School curricula aimed at building self-esteem are often good at establishing self-confidence (although much of self-confidence is determined at home before school ever begins). In addition to the self-confidence they learn at school, children can be taught by Christian parents to rely on God and others as a deterrent to the trap of self-sufficiency.

Are Schools Effective? ───────────────────────────

Critics of education focus not only on the supposed moral deterioration of schools but also on the academic deterioration. The Gablers, in *What Are They Teaching our Children?*, cite an example of an eighteen-year-old girl who was unable to count back change when she took a job as a cashier, noting she should have learned that skill in third grade. We have read newspaper accounts of high school graduates who are unable to read or write and cannot locate the United States on a world map. These distressing accounts leave us with questions about the effectiveness of public education.

Academic deterioration? Because of changing demographic characteristics, it is not an easy task to measure deterioration in schools. Rather than educating those with wealthy parents or those with unusual intelligence, American public education is egalitarian and all children have a right to a free education through twelfth grade. In many Western countries, those with the most potential, after approximately grade eight, are allowed to continue school in a college-bound program while others are diverted into vocational training programs. In the 1940s, less than half of American students completed high school. Now more than seventy-five percent complete high school. Nearly half of American youth enter college today.

When the Scholastic Aptitude Test (SAT) was introduced for the academic testing of college-bound students, few took the test because only a small proportion of high school graduates went on to college and few colleges required it. For the most part, it was the more motivated and intelligent students who went from high school into college, and their average scores were high.

As the need for education beyond high school grew, there was a corresponding increase in the number of colleges that required the SAT and an increase in the number of students who took the test. No longer was it just the intellectual elite or the wealthy who could afford college; the student population taking the SAT was now more a reflection of society at large. This change caused the average SAT scores to decline. The decline of scores was not due to a decline of the quality of education, as some have claimed, but a change in the average academic abilities of the students taking the test.

Nonetheless, there may be cause for concern. A 1983 report by the National Commission on Excellence in Education was entitled *A Nation at Risk.* The commission noted some alarming facts:

1. International comparisons of student achievement, completed a decade ago, reveal that on nineteen academic tests American students were never first or second and, in comparison with other industrialized nations, were last seven times.

2. Some twenty-three million American adults are functionally illiterate by the simplest tests of everyday reading, writing, and comprehension.

3. Average achievement of high school students on most standardized tests is now lower than twenty-six years ago when Sputnik was launched. [10]

Based on their findings, the commission recommended new basic educational goals be set with increases in English,

139

mathematics, science, social studies, and computer science. They also recommended tougher college admission standards and grading policies be adopted and that students be given more homework and a longer school year so more material can be covered. While some of their recommendations are controversial, the commission acknowledged the problem of deterioration.

Many have compared our public schools with those of other countries, especially Japan where students have the highest mathematics and science scores in the world (at least the non-Communist world). Japanese schools are also egalitarian, with ninety percent of students graduating from high school. Japanese students have fewer electives during secondary school and have longer school years and, as a result, they do better than American students in fields of science, mathematics, and social studies. Their educational results are admirable.

But in addition to reflecting education, a publication of the U.S. Department of Education suggests the success of Japanese schools also reflects their culture. Students in Japan are repeatedly taught to do their very best, and respect their teachers. In contrast, American students are less attentive to their teachers and their work. Educator Michael Kirst notes that American students talk more with classmates, wander around the room, ask unrelated questions, and stare into space. Moreover, a 1982 article in the *Journal of Educational Psychology* indicates American students spend more time playing and less time studying than Japanese or Taiwanese students. It may be unrealistic to blame the lower test scores on education because they may reflect societal differences more than educational differences.

Critical thinking. Japanese schools have their problems too. One concern is that Japanese students learn by memorization more than other methods and that memorization stifles creative thinking.

> A persistent teaching strategy in Japan is the use of imitation and rote learning — methods considered outmoded by most educators in this country . . . Japanese high school students are judged on standardized tests primarily by their memorization of facts and concepts. Japanese

teachers dispense knowledge, and the students dutifully write it down as unchallengeable truth. [11]

Even with our lower test scores, American students who learn to think critically may be better off. Educator Benjamin Bloom believes we have spent too much time on the basics, much as the Japanese have, and neglected the more significant challenges of teaching problem-solving skills. Poor problem solvers attempt to recall a memorized answer whereas creative thinkers are able to do much better.

Imagine you are a physician treating a patient with a stomach tumor. The tumor will only respond to radiation, but the dosage required will damage all the skin in the path of the radioactive beam. How will you radiate the tumor? A Gestalt psychologist created this problem to illustrate the same point Bloom makes — problem solving is more difficult than rote memory. An answer from rote memory can be given without understanding or thought. Sometimes the students with the poorest ability to memorize are the most creative in problem solving. The solution is to rotate the radioactive beam around the body with the spot of the tumor being the center point for the arc. The outlying tissue will receive less radiation, but the tumor will get the full dose.

Many critics of education argue we should return to the basics. If Benjamin Bloom is correct, it might be more important to teach skills of problem solving and creative thinking rather than spending more time on the basics.

Beyond academics. Thinking critically about education must involve thinking critically about society. Can we blame teachers and schools for poorly educated students when one-fourth of all high school students regularly smoke marijuana, more than two-thirds use alcohol, and fifteen percent have eating disorders? [12] The answer may not be to put creation back in textbooks, but may require a much more basic transformation of spiritual, social, and moral values. As Haddon Robinson pointed out in a *Christianity Today* article, we currently have more religion and less impact than in previous years. Evangelicals have demanded attention and protested inequities. Christian leaders have made the cover of *Time*, and religious books are big business, but morality in society seems

141

unaffected. Robinson concludes his article by quoting A. W. Tozer:

> It is my considered opinion that under the present circumstances we do not want revival at all. A widespread revival of the kind of Christianity we know today in America might prove to be a moral tragedy from which we would not recover in a hundred years.[13]

Educational declines may only be a symptom of broader social problems, and criticism of education may target our schools as a scapegoat for problems that go much deeper.

Thinking Critically about Public Education

Our hypothetical couple, David and Cheryl, need to use their critical thinking skills as they decide their child's schooling. They will need to consider the claims made by critics of education while looking for overgeneralizations and dichotomous thinking. Is the humanistic influence dangerous? Are academic standards deteriorating? Will my child be taught appropriate self-esteem or brainwashed with a competing atheistic religion? Parents answer these questions in various ways.

About twelve percent of parents have opted to home school their children or send them to private schools. Private schools often have smaller classrooms and specific religious orientations. But many parents cannot afford private education, and some are opposed to private education because it tends to isolate children from the real world. Also, what will happen to the public schools if all the Christian children are removed? Home schooling parents have control over the curriculum used, the daily schedule, and religious views given to their children. However, some object to home schooling because the children may lack opportunities to learn social skills and some parents are not as disciplined at giving lessons as they intended when they first decided to home school.

For those who decide on public schools, some things can be done to get good results. First, parents benefit by knowing their child's teacher. Because of antieducation books and articles, it is easy for Christians to expect the worst from teachers. Getting to know the teachers, even helping in the classroom if possible, is a good way to counter the tendency to assume the worst. Most teachers are likeable, dedicated leaders who genuinely want the best for their students. Many are Christians. Most have no hidden agendas for brainwashing children or converting them to a humanistic faith. Getting to know the teacher can alleviate fears.

Second, parents should not rely on the school to teach morality. Morality is best taught by the consistent words and example of caring parents.

> You shall therefore impress these words of mine on your heart and on your soul; and you shall bind them as a sign on your hand, and they shall be as frontals on your forehead. And you shall teach them to your sons, talking of them when you sit in your house and when you walk along the road and when you lie down and when you rise up (Deuteronomy 11:18, 19).

Rather than being upset that the school is not teaching Christian principles of morality, we need to work hard to teach morality in our homes.

Third, parents need to complement school learning with Christian learning. A study by New York University professor Paul C. Vitz indicates religious values are conspicuously missing from public school textbooks. Children who hear Christian values at church and home will be able to think and act in a Christian way despite the separation of religion and public education. Most schools hold high the values of integrity, honesty, fairness, persistence, kindness, forgiveness, and patience. Blending these values with Christian values such as prayer, obedience, worship, evangelism, service, and devotion will usually be the parents' responsibility.

143

Fourth, we need to think critically about implications of having a religious stance in the public schools. Too often we become indignant about not being able to post the Ten Commandments in the classroom before thinking through the implications of integrating religion and public education. If the Supreme Court suddenly allowed religious indoctrination back into the classroom, imagine the resulting chaos. Some teachers would post the Ten Commandments, others the Beatitudes, others passages from the Koran or the Book of Mormon. The form of religion taught would vary from district to district or school to school or teacher to teacher. Even if the Christian faith were taught, there would be diversity on doctrinal issues such as divine healing, speaking in tongues, predestination, and baptism. One thing worse than not having religion taught in public schools might be having religion taught in public schools.

CHAPTER TEN

Fears of the Crossfire

Throughout this book we have argued for critical thinking about some issues loudly debated by Christians such as the New Age Movement, positive thinking, psychology, public education, and humanism. We have pointed out the risks of not thinking critically: the vividness effect, correlation error, self-justification, freezethink, groupthink, dichotomous thinking, hasty generalizations, and seeing only what we already believe. But critical thinking also has its risks.

Standing in a crossfire is dangerous. Critical thinking sometimes requires one to question and even defy traditions and dogma in searching for truth. Like Galileo and Luther, critical thinkers are sometimes seen as offensive or heretical. Many fear critical thinking for various reasons.

The Fear of Open-mindedness

Some fear critical thinking because it seems like open-mindedness. As we discussed in Chapter 5, there are differences between open-mindedness and critical thinking. A person who is always open-minded is like a window stuck open, unable to discriminate between right and wrong, good and bad. A critical thinker is like a moveable window, and can be open to some ideas and closed to others. Consider two examples.

145

Barbara sought help because she was depressed. Her husband had left and was living with another woman, her mother had recently died, and she had just been released from her job. As she described her misfortunes, her open-mindedness stood out as a cardinal trait. Before her husband left, they had been trying to have another child. The timing was poor, however, and she discovered she was pregnant shortly after he left. She had an abortion, not because she believed in abortion, but because she "had no other choice." She was sleeping with other men within a week after her husband left. After all, her husband had been unfaithful to her so why not get back at him? Her explanation for why her husband left was that he hadn't "fooled around" during the marriage like she had. Barbara was definitely open-minded.

Tom is also open-minded. A pastor of a rapidly growing church, much of the growth comes from Tom's vital counseling ministry. People in need come to talk, and Tom demonstrates Christ's love and compassion. He is accepting of those in distress. Even his sermons communicate his care for others. Rather than criticizing the beliefs of other Christians on secondary issues, he emphasizes the unity we share in Christ. Rather than condemning sinners, he emphasizes the spiritual victories we can find in Christ and the privilege of praising God. His personal life is filled with high moral standards that others see and respect. He is an open, accepting person whose love for others causes them to experience and understand God's love.

These two cases demonstrate that receptivity to a diversity of beliefs may or may not be a part of critical thinking. In Barbara's case, nondiscriminating openness stood in the way of critical thinking. By being excessively tolerant, she actually closed her mind to greater virtue. Allan Bloom put it this way:

> Actually openness results in American conformism — out there in the rest of the world is a drab diversity that teaches only that values are relative, whereas here we can create all the life-styles we want. Our openness means we do not need others. Thus what is advertised as a great opening is a great closing. No longer is there a hope that there are great wise men in other places and times who can reveal the truth about life — except for the few remaining young people who look for a quick fix from a guru.[1]

When open-mindedness obscures virtue, it destroys morality and compromises integrity. Critical thinkers are open-minded sometimes, but they do not let their open-mindedness violate their values.

Tom, a critical thinker, models Christ's love with his blend of tolerance and firm conviction. When the Pharisees brought Jesus a woman caught in adultery, He was able to show compassion for the woman while clearly identifying her behavior as sin. Jesus concluded by affirming right values: "From now on sin no more." (John 8:11) His compassion and acceptance were balanced by His love for righteousness.

A few years ago a popular saying was, "If it feels good, do it." That's open-minded, but critical thinkers will quickly realize how ridiculous the concept is. Barbara's husband felt like having an affair, so he did. How does that fit with Paul's admonition: "Do nothing out of selfish ambition or vain conceit, but in humility consider others better than yourselves. Each of you should look not only to your own interests, but also to the interests of others" (Philippians 2:3, 4)? What if everyone felt good by cheating on taxes? What if police officers felt good about shooting drug dealers on the spot? "If it feels good, do it" is open-*mindlessness*. Excessive open-mindedness obscures truth. Karl Menninger wrote:

> It is a strange and dismal thing that in a world of such need, such opportunity and such variety as ours, the search for an illusory peace of mind should be so zealously pursued and defended, while truth goes languishing.[2]

Critical thinkers seek truth. Those who are only open-minded seek an illusory peace.

The Fear of Thought

Windows can be stuck closed just as they can be stuck open, and the closed mind is also in search of illusory peace rather than truth. Once a mind is closed to ideas because of freezethink or groupthink, there can be no more exploration or critical thinking. Both open-mindedness and closed-mindedness need to yield to critical thinking if truth is to be found. Bertrand Russell, a philosopher and critic of religion, put it this way:

> Men fear thought as they fear nothing else on earth — more than death. Thought is subversive, and revolutionary, destructive and terrible; thought is merciless to privilege, established institutions, and comfortable habits; thought is anarchic and lawless, indifferent to authority, careless to the well-tried wisdom of the ages. Thought looks into the pit of hell and is not afraid . . . . Thought is great and swift and free, the light of the world, and the chief glory of man.[3]

Some disguise closed-mindedness with the pretense of thinking. We were once asked to be part of a panel to debate whether psychology could be practiced by Christians. The panel discussion was to be moderated by a Christian talk-show host and televised nationally. As the date for the debate approached, we watched the talk show each week and became increasing uncomfortable with our upcoming appearance. The host, although claiming his show was an open debate of Christian issues, seemed to have a specific conclusion in mind before the debates ever started. Several weeks before the show, a nationally known psychologist who was to be on our side of the debate decided not to do the show because of the biases of the host. Eventually, we also backed out. It was difficult because we wanted to debate the merits of integrating Christianity and psychology, but we realized the opportunity we were given wasn't going to be a sincere search for truth.

Excessive open-mindedness is a risk, but so is excessive closed-mindedness. Critical thinking, in its best form, allows for open-mindedness in some situations and firm conviction in others. Whether one holds to a pretribulation or a post tribulation view of the return of Christ is a secondary issue of Christian doctrine, and both views have scriptural support. However, neither point of view is a test of one's orthodoxy of Bible-based Christianity. What is a test for orthodoxy is whether or not one believes that Christ will one day return. The former can be approached with a good deal of open-mindedness and the latter with firm conviction. *Lord, grant us the wisdom to be open about the nonessentials while firmly committed to the essentials. Help us actively search for truth and firmly embrace it once it is discovered.*

The Fear of Complacency

In the midst of our wealth and leisure, a frequently voiced concern about American evangelicals is that we can easily become complacent. We're concerned about what kind of new car to drive or how to best air-condition the church sanctuary, and, in the process, we neglect the millions who are malnourished and the billions who do not know Jesus. The urgencies of everyday life so easily smother the more important concerns of world evangelism and righteous living. As evangelicals in

148

America, we fight complacency. Will critical thinking contribute to complacency?

There are at least two ways to approach this problem. The first is to assume that critical thinking will lead to complacency because the mind cannot be trusted. Human reason, some argue, leads us away from obeying God. In support of this, research on human thinking indicates that we can easily delude ourselves into believing what isn't true. We tend to have more confidence in our own beliefs than is justified, and we are easily swayed to believe what is most comfortable for us to believe.

But this approach to human reason also has problems. Perhaps the biggest problem is that it assumes there is an alternative. But can we really believe or understand anything without reasoning? Our ability to think goes with us everywhere we go. Those who are complacent and those who aren't, all use their minds. A second problem with assuming that critical thinking leads to complacency is what Sigmund Freud called *neurotic anxiety* — the fear that evil will take over one's personality. One might reason, "If I trust myself and my ability to think, then I will lose my ability to control my passions and impulses." As a result, some tend to take extreme positions on issues, not because they are thinking critically, but because they fear themselves.

The television evangelist scandals provide an illustration of neurotic anxiety. When Jimmy Swaggart's sexual sin became known in February 1988, Christians remembered Swaggart's public condemnation of Jim Bakker a year earlier. Swaggart had been outspoken about the need for purity and discipline in the church. He apparently was visiting a prostitute at the same time he was condemning Bakker. Although the elements of hypocrisy cannot be denied, Swaggart probably had less hypocrisy than neurotic anxiety. When he was preaching about Bakker, he was preaching to himself, trying to motivate himself to control the immoral impulses. His rigid, dogmatic style may have been a way to defend himself against his fear of complacency.

Many Christians use this defense mechanism in similar ways. Because they fear complacency, they state positions in extreme, closed-minded ways, even while avoiding critical examination of their own lives. Some Christians who take the strongest positions against divorce are contemplating divorce in the counseling office. Their dogmatic stances cover their feelings of vulnerability.

A second way of viewing critical thinking is to see it as a tool to avoid complacency. As we evaluate our own lives critically, we can recognize our propensity toward sin and develop effective strategies to remain faithful to God. Rather than covering our fears with dogma and rigid thinking, we can attempt to honestly evaluate our fears, our motives, and our ways of thinking.

We need critical thinkers who are committed to Christian principles. Advertisements for X-rated videotapes are sent through the U.S. mail. Phone lines carry sexually explicit messages, often accessed by children and adolescents. Pay-for-service cable television channels often show perverse movies that denigrate women and men. We may be living in a sexually addicted society. It's no time for complacency. Complacency toward sin is incompatible with God's instruction through Paul:

> Therefore do not let sin reign in your mortal body so that you obey its evil desires. Do not offer the parts of your body to sin, as instruments of wickedness, but rather offer yourselves to God, as those who have been brought from death to life; and offer the parts of your body to him as instruments of righteousness. (Romans 6:12, 13)

150

There is paradox here. Those who seek happiness while avoiding critical thinking never find it. Because falling in love is fun, some become complacent to sexual sin and drift from relationship to relationship. Because having money is enjoyable, some seek money at the expense of ethics and end up morally bankrupt. Because responsibility is cumbersome, some avoid it to pursue temporal interests and end up aimlessly searching for meaning. Others seek truth through critical thinking and find happiness almost accidentally. Some commit themselves to lives of obedience and service and discover the joy of living rightly. Some discipline themselves to lives of commitment and rigor and find meaning. Truth seeking doesn't lead to complacency. If our faith is worth believing, it is worth testing with sound reason.

The Fear of Worldly Wisdom

The Apostle Paul warned the Corinthian church:

> For the message of the cross is foolishness to those who are perishing, but to us who are being saved it is the power of God. For it is written: "I will destroy the wisdom of the wise; the intelligence of the intelligent I will frustrate." (1 Corinthians 1:18, 19)

The warning is clear. Relying on human wisdom to obtain salvation from God is foolish. Some object to critical thinking because it relies so heavily on human wisdom.

This objection cannot be dismissed lightly. God's plan of grace does extend beyond human reason. Kirkegaard made a similar point in noting we can only reason to a certain point before making a "leap of faith." Faith in God cannot be reduced to critical thinking.

But to evaluate this fear it is important to distinguish different types of wisdom. In this passage, Paul is referring to a pride that places human wisdom above God's wisdom. More specifically, he is referring to those who believe they can earn God's favor and salvation. This pretentious wisdom dares to place the creature above the Creator and is dangerous and misleading. Remember that the intellectual leaders of that time were often legalistic watchdogs of the Jewish faith. The world's wisdom reduced faith to something humans could earn with intellectual understanding and adherence to a rigid set of rules.

A second kind of wisdom is that found elsewhere in the Bible. In Job, Proverbs, and Ecclesiastes we read about wisdom for living. These Scriptures are instructional for productive living and would apply well to all humans regardless of their religious faith or ideological persuasions. The proverbs in the Bible are not exclusively Christian, but they are propositions that work in the world. This wisdom is characterized by prudence, discernment, and humility.

A third kind of wisdom is specifically Christian and is found in recognizing God's plan for salvation. Today, as in the first century A.D. when Paul wrote to the Corinthians, there

151

are those who perceive God's plan for salvation as foolishness. But some are able to recognize the atoning work of Jesus Christ and to know God personally because they have been granted God's wisdom.

As Christians, we want the wisdom described in the Proverbs and the Christian wisdom that allows us to accept God's salvation, but we want to avoid the proud wisdom that places our efforts above God's grace. Critical thinking is not the "wisdom of the world" Paul is describing to the Corinthians, but the human wisdom found in Proverbs and other places in the Bible. Our fears of worldly wisdom need not be focused on critical thinking because critical thinking is a God-given gift that is advocated throughout Scripture. Our concern should be avoiding proud wisdom.

Even for us who accept God's wisdom and His plan of salvation, we sometimes struggle to keep from slipping into proud wisdom. It's difficult to accept the radical nature of God's grace. He gives something for nothing. Throughout life we learn we get what we deserve, if we work hard we will succeed. But God's message is different. "I love you regardless of what you've done." "My grace is sufficient for you." Because God's grace is so different from human reasoning, we face the battle of legalism and the battle of license.

We face battles of legalism because we cannot accept the "foolishness" of God's grace. We want to do our part, so we create actions that will make us feel more acceptable to God. Paul addressed the merits of legalism in writing to the church at Colossae:

> Since you died with Christ to the basic principles of this world, why, as though you still belonged to it, do you submit to its rules: "Do not handle! Do not taste! Do not touch!"? These are all destined to perish with use, because they are based on human commands and teachings. Such regulations indeed have an appearance of wisdom, with their self-imposed worship, their false humility and their harsh treatment of the body, but they lack any value in restraining sensual indulgence. (Colossians 2:20-23)

Extremists on one side of the crossfire seem to employ similar reasoning. "Don't play with secular toys, go to public schools, or engage in positive thinking." "Don't see a psychologist or use relaxation techniques or listen to certain kinds of music because of the backmasked messages." These prohibitions have the form of wisdom, as Paul warns, but are based on human teachings more than God's law. Legalism doesn't help in true spirituality.

The other battle caused by God's lavish grace is a battle of license. Because we are completely accepted by God, we might easily justify selfish ambition. Extremists on the other side of the crossfire seem to take positions of license. Positive thinking has been used by some to create a prosperity theology, justifying self-centered ambition. A few even suggest Christians *should* be healthy and wealthy because of God's blessing. Our proper response to God's grace is not one of selfish ambition, but of virtue and rightness.

> But if you harbor bitter envy and selfish ambition in your hearts, do not boast about it or deny the truth. Such "wisdom" does not come down from heaven but is earthly, unspiritual, of the devil. For where you have envy and selfish ambition, there you find disorder and every evil practice. But the wisdom that comes from heaven is first of all pure; then peace loving, considerate, submissive, full of mercy and good fruit, impartial and sincere. Peacemakers who sow in peace raise a harvest of righteousness. (James 3:14-18)

Critical thinking can never fully explain God's grace — that requires a leap of faith. But neither is critical thinking the wisdom of the world that Paul warns against. Christian critical thinkers watch closely to avoid proud wisdom but embrace biblical standards of human wisdom.

153

The Fear of Antisupernaturalism

Antisupernaturalists believe that God does not miraculously intervene in our world. Those who are antisupernaturalists have interpreted Scripture in a variety of ways, all emphasizing natural explanations of miracles. Antisupernaturalist Old Testament scholars, for example, have proposed that Daniel and Isaiah were written much later than commonly supposed because no one could tell the future as accurately as Daniel and Isaiah. Other scholars develop theories to account for the bodily resurrection of Jesus. Perhaps he wasn't really dead, they reason, the soldiers just thought he was dead when they removed him from the cross.

These scholars reach these conclusions because they start with an assumption that God does not do supernatural acts. Miracles, they assume, must have other explanations. Their antisupernatural worldview affects the way they interpret Scripture.

Those with antisupernatural assumptions often use good critical thinking skills, but their conclusions reflect their assumptions or presuppositions as much as their abilities to think critically. *Critical thinking is a process, not a set of right or wrong conclusions.* Two critical thinkers will often come to different conclusions because they each began with different assumptions.

Evangelical Christians begin with the assumption that God transcends nature and is able to perform miracles that contradict natural law. Based on this assumption, we interpret biblical miracles as they are recorded. However, we can still think critically within the boundaries of our assumptions.

Our assumptions are based on faith and reason. Accepting that God intervenes supernaturally requires a step of faith, but even that step of faith can be buttressed by critical thinking. Christians look to those who have been healed of disease or those whose financial needs have been miraculously met at the last minute as evidence of supernatural intervention. Similarly, believing God does not intervene supernaturally requires faith. Antisupernaturalists notice the Christians who aren't healed from disease or those who go bankrupt as they wait for God's intervention. Both groups think critically and come to different conclusions.

Critical thinking need not lead one to antisupernaturalism. In fact, critical thinking is the best way to remain committed to our positions of faith. Imagine you have doubts about the existence of God, as most Christians do from time to time. If there is no God, from where did you come? From your parents of course. From where did your parents, grandparents, and other ancestors come? From monkeys of course. From where did the monkeys come? From amoebas of course. From where did the amoebas come? From methane gas. How did we get the methane gas? From the big bang fueled by other gases. You get the point. This sequence of questions can go forever. But eventually you either have to believe in the eternal existence of matter or the eternal existence of God who created the matter. It seems more reasonable to conclude God has always existed than to conclude matter has always existed. In this case, critical thinking supported the position of faith. It need not lead one to the assumption of antisupernaturalism.

The Solution: Critical Thinking Requires Balance _____

Imagine a battlefield. While opponents are exchanging shots, a few bystanders are walking around in the midst of the crossfire looking for buried treasure. Looking for truth is sometimes as threatening. The Bible is filled with truth, psychologists have some truth, Dave Hunt has some truth, the hippies had some truth, the yuppies have some truth, humanists have some truth, Norman Vincent Peale has some truth, and public educators have some truth. As we walk around the battlefield searching for the truth, we are likely to be attacked by one side or the other. Critical thinking is not for cowards.

Living in the crossfire is dangerous. Whether we think critically or not, there is the potential for us to lose our sense of balance, to become excessively open-minded or closed-minded, to become complacent, to err toward legalism or license. Keeping balance is a delicate task, helped by asking several probing questions.

Question 1: Am I open to being wrong? We all tend to overestimate the accuracy of our beliefs. We sometimes assume we are right even in the presence of contradictory evidence, pushing us toward closed-mindedness and legalism. Critical thinkers must have a healthy fear of invalidity and consider the possibility that they are wrong.

A Christian expert on the cults once asked an audience of Mormons if they would abandon their faith if he could prove that Joseph Smith was a fraud. Many said they would not abandon their faith, even if Smith was proven to be a fraud. We smile with contempt at such rigid thinking, but sometimes we may be equally guilty.

What about creation? What if irrefutable evidence turns up tomorrow that the theory of evolution is correct? Would

155

we be able to abandon literal creationism and still affirm God's presence in history? Remember that the church of Galileo's day believed the Bible only supported an earth-centered view of the universe.

Question 2: Do my prior opinions hinder my commitment to truth? Firm beliefs are good, allowing us to make decisions quickly and consistently. But when those beliefs become excessively rigid, they can hinder our pursuit of truth. This is especially true in the context of a group where groupthink solidifies the beliefs of group members, making them resistant to considering contradictory evidence. Firm conviction must be balanced with a willingness to seek truth.

Conversely, one can be so accepting of new ideas that he or she does not form firm convictions, resulting in a life devoid of values. Moral decisions become difficult because there is not a well-defined ethical structure to use to make tough choices. In these cases, our thinking processes are especially prone to self-justification. Open-mindedness must be balanced by a commitment to truth.

Question 3: Am I leaving room for God to be God? As we think critically, it is important to humbly embrace our human limitations. Even the best critical thinkers are prone to overconfidence and distortion. So we must leave room for God to correct us through Scripture, the thoughts of others, and the guidance of the Holy Spirit. God gave us the ability to think critically (human wisdom) and instructed us to use it responsibly to know Him and His world better. It must grieve God when His created beings believe they know more than their Creator. Paul warned of idolatry stemming from supposed wisdom:

156

> For although they knew God, they neither glorified him as God nor gave thanks to him, but their thinking became futile and their foolish hearts were darkened. Although they claimed to be wise, they became fools and exchanged the glory of the immortal God for images made to look like mortal man and birds and animals and reptiles. (Romans 1:21-23)

When human reason becomes god and obscures spiritual understanding, we exchange truth for human arrogance.

Christian critical thinking leaves room for God to be God – it can help us understand Him better.

CHAPTER ELEVEN

Christ-centered Vision

When we play darts, the wall suffers. Why don't they make dart boards bigger? Walls in college dormitories often look like a woodpecker's playground with a dartboard hanging in the middle. Hitting the dime-sized bull's-eye in the center of the board seems impossible.

Hitting the bull's-eye with our lives, honoring Christ with our words, thoughts, and actions, is also difficult. There are so many things to keep in mind — job demands, family responsibilities, helping those in need, church involvement, financial obligations, and so on. All around us people miss the bull's-eye with their lives and eventually die, only making a mark on the wall holding the target.

Jesus Christ is the essence of Christianity. Because of His life, death, and resurrection we have hope and life in Him. The author of Hebrews, after describing the heroes of faith who hit the bull's-eye, wrote:

> Therefore, since we are surrounded by such a great cloud of witnesses, let us throw off everything that hinders and the sin that so easily entangles, and let us run with perseverance the race marked out for us. Let us fix our eyes on Jesus, the author and perfector of our faith, who for the joy set before him endured the cross, scorning its shame, and sat down at the right hand of the throne of God. (Hebrews 12:1, 2)

157

As we fix our eyes on Jesus, we see things in their proper perspective. Christ-centered vision is the goal of the Christian life. Even as he was in prison facing death, Paul considered "everything a loss compared to the surpassing greatness of knowing Christ Jesus . . . ." (Philippians 3:8)

Visual Cataracts

Our vision is to be set on Christ—He is our target. But our vision is so easily distorted. It is clouded by the cataracts of self-interest. Throughout this book we have suggested different ways our thinking is distorted. In each case, we all tend to overestimate the value of our opinions, to filter reality through a self-centered focus. Sometimes these patterns are worsened by group or time pressures, as in groupthink and freezethink. Doing our thinking in a group context does not always clear up our distorted vision.

During the period when the Israelites were governed by judges, they repeatedly turned their backs on God. God punished them and showed kindness to them each time, and they returned for a short while. But even in the context of a group where they could support and remind each other about God's law, they turned their backs again. The cycle repeated many times as the Israelites were distracted by the pleasures and responsibilities of their world. Their self-centered biases occurred even with God's frequent reminders and with the support of a group of like-minded people.

Our vision can also be distorted while fighting for good causes. Much of the crossfire described in this book is caused by well-meaning Christians who want to honor God with their lives but have failed to see the fallacies in their own arguments. In the midst of the ideological crossfire, many have convinced themselves that they see things more clearly than others and that they must purify the church.

158

Keeping the church pure is important, but it is not the bull's-eye of the Christian life, it is only a tool allowing us to enter into a deeper faith and commitment to Christ. Following Christ, honoring Him with our lives, and living as He would have us live is a higher calling. When zeal for correcting others interferes with our vision for Christ, we need to beware.

Another way our vision can be distorted is by focusing on legalistic symbols that have been associated with Christianity. Sometimes we value a list of approved and disapproved behaviors more than our relationship with Jesus Christ. We do well to remember Paul's words about legalism:

> Therefore do not let anyone judge you by what you eat or drink, or with regard to a religious festival, a New Moon celebration or a Sabbath day. These are a shadow of the things that were to come; *the reality, however, is found in Christ.* (Colossians 2:16, 17)

Paul is not suggesting that celebrations or Sabbaths are unimportant, but that they are not essential for salvation. They are not the bull's-eye of Christian living. We no longer fight about festivals, or New Moons or Sabbath days, but over relaxation techniques, public education, self-esteem, and psychological counseling. Paul's point still applies. These issues need to be carefully considered, but they are not the basis of our salvation or the essence of a Christ-centered vision. The reality is found in Christ.

Loving God with Our Minds

The greatest commandment, according to Jesus, is to "love the Lord your God with all your heart and with all your soul and with all your mind." (Matthew 22:37) It is an act of stewardship to train our minds to think critically. The Apostle Peter instructed:

> But in your hearts set apart Christ as Lord. Always be prepared to give an answer to everyone who asks you to give the reason for the hope that you have. But do this with gentleness and respect, keeping a clear conscience, so that those who speak maliciously against your good behavior in Christ may be ashamed of their slander. (1 Peter 3:15, 16)

159

We are to think critically without being critical people. Being prepared to defend our faith involves the ability to think clearly about issues of great importance, but Peter also emphasized our need to be gentle. This gentleness can coexist with critical thinking as we allow Christ to transform our lives and modify our self-centered biases and unnecessary dogma.

Purity of focus. Loving God with our minds implies a purity of focus in our thinking. Although we can think critically about a variety of issues, our thinking is rooted in devotion to Christ. The Apostle Paul said it well, writing to the Philippians:

But whatever was to my profit I now consider loss for the sake of Christ. What is more, I consider everything a loss compared to the surpassing greatness of knowing Christ Jesus my Lord, for whose sake I have lost all things. I consider them rubbish, that I may gain Christ and be found in him, not having a righteousness of my own that comes from the law, but that which is through faith in Christ— the righteousness that comes from God and is by faith. I want to know Christ and the power of his resurrection and the fellowship of sharing in his sufferings, becoming like him in his death, and so, somehow, to attain to the resurrection from the dead. (Philippians 3:7-10)

Critical thinkers who have Christ-centered focus don't take pleasure in shaming other believers because of doctrinal differences. If we make unreasonable attacks on fellow believers, we are elevating ourselves above others and missing the bull's-eye with our critical thinking. In fact, the goal Paul describes is forgetting ourselves as we focus on Christ and His power.

A responsibility to question. Even those with purity of focus disagree on some issues. And when faced with disagreement, those who are gentle and Christ-centered are willing to boldly confront the issues. It is never more spiritual just to believe something than it is to question before believing. Part of loving God with our minds is accepting the responsibility to question others, as evidenced by the actions of Jesus.

Jesus questioned the traditions of His day, allowing His disciples to eat grain from the field (Mark 2:23-28), healing a man's withered hand (Mark 3:1-6) on the Sabbath, and eating with tax collectors and "sinners." His teaching was radical, but He modeled independent, critical thinking. Rather than blindly conforming to the traditions of the culture, He thought freely and came to sound conclusions.

Loving God with our minds involves thinking critically about the difficult questions of life. We have a responsibility to question the answers given by others, just as Jesus questioned the traditional answers of His day.

Christians also have a responsibility to question simplistic spiritual explanations. In New Testament times, the Pharisees had taken the biblical commandment too far and had converted the Sabbath into a day of legalistic passivity. Jesus questioned the simplistic standard. But Jesus did more than just question the Pharisees' beliefs about the Sabbath. He challenged them with difficult questions and Scripture. Questioning is not enough. We also need to seek truth by searching Scripture, thinking critically, and seeking God's guidance.

Thought liberates Christians from the oppression of unsupported dogma and simplistic solutions. It allows us to approach God directly, using our own minds rather than traditions of the Church or religious leaders. Thought allows us to love God freely with our minds. Of course we need others to help us recognize when we are thinking clearly, but we each have a personal responsibility before God to love Him by thinking about His commandments and His world.

A grounding for our faith. Loving God with our minds allows us to ground our faith in reason. Faith not rooted in reason is vulnerable to persuasive speech, changing emotions, and philosophical fads. How do we ground our faith in reason?

First, we study and contemplate God's special revelation. By reading and understanding God's Word we understand more about Him and His creation.

> Blessed is the man who does not walk in the counsel of the wicked or stand in the way of sinners or sit in the seat of mockers. But his delight is in the law of the Lord, and on his law he meditates day and night. He is like a tree planted by streams of water, which yields its fruit in season and whose leaf does not wither. Whatever he does prospers. (Psalm 1:1-3)

161

Understanding the Bible also helps us sort out the arguments of others. When authors begin their book titles with "The biblical view of . . ." critical thinkers can compare the content with their own knowledge of Scripture. Some write books on the biblical reasons for self-esteem while others write on how the Bible argues against self-esteem. Only by studying Scripture ourselves and reading books on both sides can we come to personal convictions about the issues currently facing Christians. One of the beautiful things about the Bible is that we all can understand it. We need not let scholars do all the interpreting for us, although their work often helps us reach right conclusions.

A second way we ground our faith in reason is by studying God's general revelation. We, like Galileo, can discover truth by investigating God's world. For some this means research in the chemistry laboratory, for others, reading classical literature or appreciating good music and art. As we study God's world we learn more about His truth.

One example of studying God's general revelation is seen in this book. Many of the principles of critical thinking discussed come from developments in social and cognitive psychology. These truths, discovered by social scientists, can help us better understand God as we ground our faith in reason.

A third way we ground our faith in reason is by living in simple obedience. A growing body of social psychology literature indicates that we form our beliefs based on our actions. We act and then form our attitudes based on what we see ourselves doing. This is dangerous because we easily justify our actions by changing our beliefs.

Blind obedience is not the goal. Jesus restored a man's hand because He was willing to question the prevailing Sabbath standards. It is good to question why we believe and why we obey. But when disobedience is selfish or emotionally appealing, we cannot trust our reason alone.

A fourth way to ground our faith in reason, one we have emphasized throughout this book, is to explore both sides of issues. In trying to convince readers that psychology is ineffective, William Kilpatrick, Martin and Deidre Bobgan, and Dave Hunt cite a few studies that support their position that psychology doesn't work. They selectively ignore the hundreds of studies showing clinical psychology is effective. By presenting only one side of the issue, they hope to bring readers to their way of thinking. Grounding our faith in reason involves looking for true understanding and not settling for lopsided information.

A commitment to godliness. Loving God with our minds also requires committing ourselves — morally, intellectually, and volitionally — to godliness. This is a natural response to Christ-centered critical thinking.

Behavior almost always involves the mind. If a father instructs his daughter to cover her mouth when she coughs, and she obeys, there are several cognitive events that must occur. First, she needs to *understand* the instruction. A six-month-old might smile or spit up in her father's face, but she certainly would not understand the instructions to cover her mouth. Second, the coughing daughter will need to *remember* the instructions next time the urge for a cough comes. Finally, she needs to *know how to modify* her behavior to respond appropriately. To obey she must use her thinking skills. Similarly, to obey God we must depend on our thinking abilities.

Too often we approach godliness as a motivational issue. Some pastors fill their sermons with motivational rhetoric. Their congregations are touched, tears flow freely, and altar calls are successful. But often listeners have no new understanding or knowledge. They may be motivated to change, but they haven't learned *how* to change.

Other pastors are skilled at teaching thinking skills because they realize thinking skills are necessary for permanent change. Rather than inducing motivation or guilt, they teach in ways that inspire thinking. Thinking is powerful, and right thinking is a catalyst for godliness.

Both kinds of pastors have something to offer. We need to be motivated and emotions are often useful as motivating forces. But we also need to know how to change, and careful thought and rationality is essential for us to produce real change in our lives.

Commitment to godliness requires careful thinking and cannot be reduced to spiritual reflex. Although strongly oriented toward godliness and obedience, Christian fundamentalism, with its extrabiblical legalism and politics, sometimes borders on reflexive spirituality. Some former fundamentalists have bound together to form Fundamentalists Anonymous (FA), an organization fighting guilt, self-doubt, and intolerance. Founder Dr. Richard Yao targets the fundamentalist addiction as "inability to tolerate ambiguity and uncertainty in life; its inclination to paint everything in black and white, right and wrong, good and evil."[1] I like Joseph Bayley's conclusion about FA, that he doesn't mind them giving up fundamentalism, but he hopes they don't give up Christ. "Christianity is Christ, not fundamentalism."[2]

Painting everything as black or white, right or wrong, appeals to a sense of simplicity, but many issues cannot be reduced to such a reflexive system of ethics. King David took consecrated bread to feed his men even though it was only for priests to eat (1 Samuel 21). Jesus intervened for a woman about to be stoned for adultery though the law clearly stated she should be put to death (John 8). The reflexive answers aren't always right.

Some Christians advocate political reflexiveness as well. The watchdogs of the faith want us to vote according to their prescription. If not specifically stated, they imply that committed Christians should feel and vote certain ways on issues. This removes our responsibility to think through issues and come to individual conclusions before God. The commitment to godliness requires careful thought and evaluation and can never be adequately reduced to reflex.

Searching for Meaning

Psychiatrist Victor Frankl was imprisoned in a Nazi concentration camp during World War II. Being a student of human experience, he analyzed and recorded his own experiences during those traumatic years of captivity. After his release, when he discovered his wife and children were dead, he wrote books on the human search for meaning. Finding meaning, according to Frankl, is the voyage of life.

As Christians, we have found meaning. Jesus Christ has redeemed us and freed us from the bondage of selfish existence. But our search goes on. As we love Christ with our minds, we search for greater understanding, not being content with simplistic answers or lopsided arguments. Paul Tournier puts it well:

> To seek the meaning of things and God's will does not spare us either from error or from doubt; nor does it solve all the mysteries of our destiny, all the insoluble problems which are set us by any event of Nature or in our lives; nevertheless, it does give a new meaning in our lives.[3]

Sometimes our search for meaning requires us to stand firm in the midst of crossfire. Those on both flanks want to take us captive, to have us believe as they believe, sometimes without questioning.

As we love God with our minds we can think freely, read widely, investigate boldly, and obey consistently. Some critical thinkers join one flank or the other, but they walk there on their own initiative, fully aware of the issues and arguments that arm the other side and always with a Christ-centered vision.

Notes

Chapter 1 ───────────────────────────

. 1 Earl D. Radmacher, *You and Your Thoughts: The Power of Right Thinking* (Wheaton, Ill.: Tyndale House, 1977), 8.

2 Dave Hunt and T. A. McMahon, *The Seduction of Christianity: Spiritual Discernment in the Last Days* (Eugene, Ore.: Harvest House, 1985), 131.

3 Tim LaHaye, *The Battle for the Mind* (Old Tappan, N.J.: Fleming H. Revell, 1980), 9.

4 Constance Cumbey, *The Hidden Dangers of the Rainbow* (Shreveport, La.: Huntington House, 1983), 18.

5 Edgar C. Whisenant, *On Borrowed Time* (Nashville: World Bible Society, 1988).

6 David A. Noebel, *The Marxist Minstrels: A Handbook on Communist Subversion of Music* (Tulsa: American Christian College Press, 1974), p.i.

7 Cumbey, *The Hidden Dangers of the Rainbow*, 28.

8 Phil Phillips, *Turmoil in the Toybox* (Lancaster: Starburst, 1986), 79.

9 LaHaye, *The Battle for the Mind*, 95.

10 Ibid., 10.

11 William Kirk Kilpatrick, *Psychological Seduction: The Failure of Modern Psychology* (New York: Thomas Nelson, 1983).

12 Dave Hunt and T. A. McMahon, *America: The Sorcerer's New Apprentice* (Eugene, Ore.: Harvest House, 1988), 131.

13 Jimmy Swaggart, "Christian Psychology?" *The Evangelist* (November 1986), 4-9.

14 Dave Hunt, *Beyond Seduction: A Return to Biblical Christianity* (Eugene, Ore.: Harvest House, 1987), 128.

15 Cumbey, *The Hidden Dangers of the Rainbow*, 42.

16 Douglas R. Groothuis, *Unmasking the New Age* (Downers Grove, Ill.: InterVarsity Press, 1986), 34.

Chapter 2 ───────────────────────────

1 David Hothersall, *History of Psychology* (New York: Random House, 1984), 23.

2 Martin and Deidre Bobgan, *Psychoheresy* (Santa Barbara: Eastgate, 1987), 32.

3 Bruce A. Demarest, *General Revelation: Historical Views and Contemporary Issues* (Grand Rapids: Zondervan, 1982), 16.

4 Dave Hunt, *Beyond Seduction: A Return to Biblical Christianity* (Eugene, Ore.: Harvest House, 1987), 127-128.

5 Ibid., 134.

6 "Christian Toys Offer Alternative," *The Sunday Oregonian* (August 10, 1986).

7 Tim LaHaye, *The Battle for the Mind* (Old Tappan, N.J.: Fleming H. Revell, 1980), 95.

8 Charles Krauthammer, "The Humanist Phantom," *New Republic* (July 25, 1981), 21.

9 John Baker, "Fundamentalism as Anti-intellectualism," *The Humanist* Vol. 40, No. 2 (1986) 28.

10 Ibid., 26.

11 Bobgan, *Psychoheresy*, 34.

12 Dave Hunt and T. A. McMahon, *America: The Sorcerer's New Apprentice* (Eugene, Ore.: Harvest House, 1988), 126.

13 G. C. Scipione and E. Payne, eds., *The Christian World View of Psychology and Counseling* (Mountain View, Calif.: The Coalition on Revival, Inc., 1986), 6-7.

14 Pope John Paul II, cited in Hothersall, *History of Psychology*, 24.

Chapter 3

1 David Meyers, *Psychology* (New York: Worth, 1986), 560.

2 Daryl and Sandra Bem, "Homogenizing the American Woman: The Power of an Unconscious Ideology," *Contemporary Issues in Social Psychology*, 3rd ed., eds. Brugham and Wrightman (Monterey, Ca.: Brooks Cole, 1977), 181-182.

3 Mel and Norma Gabler, *What Are They Teaching Our Children?* (Wheaton: Victor, 1985).

4 Phil Phillips, *Turmoil in the Toybox* (Lancaster: Starburst, 1986), 36-37.

5 Robert A. Schuller, *How to Be an Extraordinary Person in an Ordinary World* (Old Tappan, N.J.: Fleming H. Revel, 1985).

6 William Kirk Kilpatrick, *Psychological Seduction: The Failure of Modern Psychology* (New York: Thomas Nelson, 1983), 13.

7 Constance Cumbey, *The Hidden Dangers of the Rainbow* (Shreveport, La.: Huntington House, 1983), 18.

8 Kilpatrick, *Psychological Seduction: The Failure of Modern Psychology*, 31.

9 Gabler, *What Are They Teaching Our Children?*, 73.

10 Leon Festinger, Henry Riecken and Stanley Schachter, *When Prophecy Fails* (Minneapolis: University of Minnesota, 1956).

11 Cumbey, *The Hidden Dangers of the Rainbow*, 23.

12 Festinger, *When Prophecy Fails*, 6-22.

13 Robert Rosenthal and Lenore Jacobson, *Pygmalion in the Classroom: Teacher Expectation and Pupils' Intellectual Development* (New York: Holt, Rinehart, & Winston, 1968).

14 David L. Rosenhan and Martin E. Seligman, *Abnormal Psychology* (New York: Norton, 1984), 607.

15 C. Cannell and J. MacDonald, "The Impact of Health News on Attitude and Behavior," *Journalism Quarterly* (1956), 315-323.

16 William Thornton, "The New Nonsectarian Right," *The Humanist*, Vol. 46, No. 30 (January/February 1986), 30.

17 Cumbey, *The Hidden Dangers of the Rainbow*, 24.

18 Gabler, *What Are They Teaching Our Children?* 47.

19 Douglas R. Groothius, *Unmasking the New Age* (Downers Grove, Ill.: InterVarsity Press, 1986), 190.

20 *Scientific American* (December 1922), 389.

21 Charles Edward Mark Hansel, *ESP and Parapsychology: A Critical Reevaluation* (Buffalo: Prometheus, 1980), 314.

22 David Meyers, *Social Psychology* (New York: McGraw-Hill, 1983), 165.

Chapter 4

1 Arie W. Kruglanski, "Freeze-Think and the Challenger," *Psychology Today* (August 1986), 48-49.

2 Irving L. Janis, "Groupthink," *Psychology Today* (November 1971), 46.

3 Ibid., 46-47.

4 Edward McNulty, "Taming the TV Habit," *Christian Herald* (September 1986), 24.

5 Elliot Aronson, *The Social Animal*, 5th ed. (New York: W. H. Freeman, 1988), 57.

6 Clayton Lafferty and Alonzo Pond, *The Desert Survival Situation* (Plymouth, Mich.: Human Synergistics, 1974).

169

Chapter 5

1 Timothy Sims, "Learning from the Fundamentalists," *The Christian Century* (1985), 1140-1141.

2 Kenneth Feder, "Spooks, Spirits, and College Students," *The Humanist* (May/June 1985), 17, 18.

3 David Myers, *Psychology* (New York: Worth, 1986), 420.

4 Allan Bloom, *The Closing of the American Mind* (New York: Simon and Schuster, 1987), 26.

5 Ibid., 56-57.

6 Martin and Deidre Bobgan, *Psychoheresy* (Santa Barbara: Eastgate, 1987), 7.

7 William Law, *The Power of the Spirit*. ed. Dave Hunt (Fort Washington: Christian Literature Crusade, 1971), 52. Quoted in Bobgan, *Psychoheresy*, 34-35.

8 Thomas Leahey, *A History of Psychology* (Englewood Cliffs, N.J.: Prentice Hall, 1980), 58.

9 Tim LaHaye, *The Battle for the Mind* (Old Tappan, N.J.: Fleming H. Revell, 1980), 27.

10 William Kirk Kilpatrick, *Psychological Seduction: The Failure of Modern Psychology* (Nashville: Thomas Nelson, 1983), 30.

11 Daniel Taylor, *The Myth of Certainty* (Waco, Tex.: Word Books, 1986), 9-10

12 Ibid., 14

13 Kenneth Kinghorn, "Q & A: The Care Bear Controversy", *The Asbury Herald* (Spring, 1988), 12.

14 Ibid., 12.

15 Dave Hunt, *Beyond Seduction: A Return to Biblical Christianity* (Eugene, Ore.: Harvest House, 1987), 17.

16 Ibid., 114.

Chapter 6

1 Norman Vincent Peale, *The Power of Positive Thinking* (New York: Fawcett Crest, 1956), 176.

2 Robert H. Schuller, *Move Ahead with Possibility Thinking* (Old Tappan, N.J.: Fleming H. Revell, 1967), 145.

3 Norman Vincent Peale, *The Power of Positive Thinking*, 23.

4 Robert H. Schuller, *Move Ahead with Possibility Thinking*, 14-15.

5 Norman Vincent Peale, *The Power of Positive Thinking*, 23.

6 Robert H. Schuller, *How to be an Extraordinary Person in an Ordinary World* (Old Tappan, N.J.: Fleming H. Revell, 1985), 170.

7 Norman Vincent Peale, *The Power of Positive Thinking*, 23.

8 Ibid., 27.

9 John Throop, "High Hopes: What's Wrong (and Right) with Ambition," *Christianity Today* (October 3, 1986), 24-25.

10 Dave Hunt, *Beyond Seduction: A Return to Biblical Christianity* (Eugene, Ore.: Harvest House, 1987), 47.

11 Dave Hunt, "Old Lies from the New Age," *The Chosen People* (June 1988), 4-10.

12 Havelock Ellis in *The Dance of Life.* Cited in George Seldes (Ed.), *The Great Thoughts* (New York: Ballantine Books, 1985), 125.

13 Cited in David Myers and Malcolm Jeeves, *Psychology: Through the Eyes of Faith* (San Francisco: Harper & Row, 1987), 140.

14 Ibid., 130-133.

Chapter 7

1 An abridged version of this chapter first appeared as an article, "The Mind Doctors," *Christianity Today* (April 8, 1988).

2 Paul C. Vitz, *Psychology as Religion: The Cult of Self-worship* (Grand Rapids, Mich.: Eerdmans, 1977).

3 Martin and Deidre Bobgan, *The Psychological Way/The Spiritual Way* (Minneapolis, Minn.: Bethany House Publishers, 1977).

4 Jimmy Swaggart, "Christian Psychology?" *The Evangelist* (November 1986), 4-9.

5 William Kirk Kilpatrick and Robert Roberts, *Christianity Today* (November 8, 1985), 20-24.

Chapter 8

1 Cited in Homer Duncan, *Secular Humanism: The Most Dangerous Religion in America* (Lubbock, Tex.: Christian Focus on Government, Inc., 1979), 11.

2 Tim LaHaye, *The Battle for the Mind* (Old Tappan, N.J.: Fleming H. Revell, 1980), 30.

3 Ibid., 136.

4 Henry K. Misiak and Virginia Staudt Sexton, *Phenomenological, Existential, and Humanistic Psychologies: A Historical Survey* (New York: Grune and Stratton, 1973), 116.

5 Abraham Maslow, "The Instinctoid Nature of Human Needs," *Journal of Personality*, 22 (1954) 326.

6 Richard B. Cunningham, "Christianity and Contemporary Humanism," *Review and Expositor*, 81 (1984), 281.

7 Ibid., 277.

8 Dave Hunt and T. A. McMahon, *The Seduction of Christianity: Spiritual Discernment in the Last Days* (Eugene, Ore.: Harvest House, 1985), 193.

9 Duncan, *Secular Humanism: The Most Dangerous Religion in America*, 19.

10 George Albee, "Preventing Psychopathology and Promoting Human Potential," *American Psychologist*, 37 (1982), 1049.

11 Duncan, *Secular Humanism: The Most Dangerous Religion in America*, 19.

171

Chapter 9

1 *How to Understand Humanism* (Institute of Basic Youth Conflicts, 1983), 3.

2 Alfred North Whitehead, *The Aims of Education* (New York: Mentor Books, 1929).

3 "Connecticut Mutual Life Report," *Family Concern*, ed. J. Allan Peterson (Wheaton, Ill.).

4 *How to Understand Humanism* (Institute of Basic Youth Conflicts, 1983), 3.

5 Tim LaHaye, *The Battle for the Mind* (Old Tappan, N.J.: Fleming H. Revell, 1980), 57.

6 Justice Clark in 1963 Supreme Court decision, "Abington School District v. Schempp," *How to Understand Humanism* (Institute of Basic Youth Conflicts, 1983), 3.

7 Ronald J. Miller, "The Meanings of Education," *The Humanist* (March/April, 1984), 15.

8 Mel and Norma Gabler, *What Are They Teaching Our Children?* (Wheaton, Ill.: Victor Books, 1985).

9 Mark McMinn and James Foster, "The Humanism Attitude Scale: Analyzing a Straw Person" (Poster presented at the annual meetings of the Western Psychological Association, San Francisco, April 1988).

10 *A Nation at Risk* (Washington, D.C.: U.S. Government Printing Office, 1983), 8-9.

11 Michael Kirst, *Who Controls Our Schools?* (Stanford, Cal.: Stanford Alumni Association, 1984), 86-87.

12 "Human Statistics," *Infochange* (October 1986), 7.

13 Haddon Robinson, "More Religion, Less Impact," *Christianity Today* (January 17, 1986), 41-51.

Chapter 10

1 Allan Bloom, *The Closing of the American Mind* (New York: Simon & Schuster, 1987), 34.

2 Karl Menninger in *This Week* (October 16, 1958).

3 Bertrand Russell in *Education and the Good Life* (1926) cited in George Seldes (Ed.), *The Great Thoughts* (New York: Ballantine Books, 1985), 361-362.

Chapter 11

1 Cited in Joseph Bayley, "They'd Rather Switch Than Fight," *Eternity* (March 1986), 80.

2 Ibid., 80.

3 Paul Tournier, *A Doctor's Casebook* (San Francisco: Harper & Row, 1976), 37.

Glossary

Cognitive: Having to do with thinking. Cognitive structure is the need to have a clear way of thinking about an issue. Cognitive psychotherapy focuses on changing behaviors and feelings by changing ways of thinking.

Correlation Error: Assuming because two events are related, that one causes the other. Actually, the two events may be related for any number of reasons. For example, hours of television viewing and childhood obesity are related. But we cannot conclude that television watching causes obesity because it is equally possible that obese children are more likely to enjoy television or that some third variable causes both obesity and television watching. Correlation does not prove cause and effect.

Critical Thinking: The discipline of looking for alternative explanations rather than assuming an obvious conclusion or the conclusion of another is valid. Critical thinkers are able to check ideas with observations, or observations against other data, skeptically investigating before assuming something is true. Critical thinking includes a humble awareness of our human tendency to think in erroneous and self-serving ways.

173

Dichotomous Thinking: Impeding critical thinking by thinking in all-or-none terms. For example, a dichotomous thinker may conclude, "If I don't succeed at everything I attempt, then I am a complete failure." Categories of speech often push us toward dichotomous thinking. We hear of winners and losers, successes and failures, love and hate. Thinking in extreme all-or-none ways produces troubling emotions and prevents critical thinking.

Freezethink: A thinking pattern that values decisions over prolonged discussion and consideration. Those experiencing freezethink prefer the psychological comfort of any decision to the discomfort of indecision, thus prematurely cutting off the decision-making process.

General Revelation: God making Himself known through His creation. Human endeavors such as science and humanities are ways of knowing God's world better, and since God reveals Himself through His creation, ways of knowing God better.

Groupthink: The kind of thinking that can occur when a group of people value agreement with each other so highly that they cannot see the flaws in the decision-making process. The group experiencing groupthink can become so cohesive and the members so protective of the group and the group leader, that differing points of view are actively discouraged.

Hasty Generalization: Coming to a general, categorical conclusion before considering all the relevant information. Someone once said, "All Indians walk single file; at least the one I saw did." Hasty generalization is the basis for prejudice and stifles critical thinking.

Humanism: A system of thought that emphasizes the freedom and dignity of humankind. Humanists see men and women as creative, self-directed, and good. Humanism is a diverse philosophical system and its proponents hold a variety of differing beliefs. Some humanists are atheistic while others believe God ordained human freedom and goodness.

Invalidity: Coming to a wrong conclusion. Having an inadequate fear of invalidity results in people coming to decisions prematurely, before considering the consequences of a poor decision or conclusion.

174

New Age Movement: A worldwide pantheistic religious movement of over 3,500 groups and organizations. New Agers believe in reincarnation, that their previous and present lives lead to a cosmic destiny that will be fulfilled by achieving greater understanding and awareness. Their goal is to bring enlightenment to humankind—the Age of Aquarius. Based on astrology, they believe changes will gradually take place between 1984 and 2020 until our planet is aligned with Aquarius.

Open-mindedness: The willingness to consider alternative perspectives before coming to definite conclusions. Open-mindedness allows for critical thinking, but it is important not to value open-mindedness so highly that one never comes to conclusions.

Proof-texting: Using a Bible passage or other text to support one's opinions even though the context of the text is intended for a different application or meaning. This gives one's opinions a false authority because the supporting text is being used inaccurately or is out of context.

Secular Humanism: A nontheistic worldview that does not consider supernatural explanations for human potential or behavior. Secular humanists believe that all human achievement is the result of the human mind and human effort, and that the problems facing humankind will be solved through human effort.

Self-justification: The self-deception pattern where people find reasons to justify or excuse their behaviors and opinions. Even though we perceive ourselves to act according to our well-reasoned beliefs, we often act or believe first, then develop reasons for our beliefs and actions.

Special Revelation: God making Himself known through Scripture. In addition to His general revelation through creation, God has given us specific instruction and information in the Bible. Christians differ on their recognition of other forms of special revelation, such as personally receiving God's instruction.

175

Vividness Effect: A specific vivid example that causes people to overestimate the validity or frequency of a problem or occurrence. This is sometimes called the availability heuristic. Those memories which are most available are likely to be seen as more common than they actually are.